What they never told you about RE

Owen F. Cummings
Bristol, 25-1-82

TERENCE COPLEY &
DONALD EASTON

What they
never told you
about RE

SCM PRESS LTD

334 01773 4

First published 197
by SCM Press Ltd
56 Bloomsbury Stre , London

© SCM Press Ltd 974

Printed in Great B itain by
Northumberland ress Limited
Gateshead

To the Hidden Man

Contents

Contents

Preface

This is a curious book. We hope it will appeal to those who haven't been 'turned on' by RE in the past; we hope it gives a picture of what RE can be like and an insight into recent developments. It doesn't originate from the ivory tower but rather from the shop floor of our own experience; the critically hostile reviewer is invited to get into the classroom and have a go himself.

This is not intended as a textbook in the traditional sense – a systematic, exhaustive (and usually exhausting) study. We think of it as a series of parables, pictures of particular situations in RE in a particular context, but having wider application. An index is added, however, so that people in search of information on specific topics can trace the relevant sections more easily.

Our strong views about the RE situation can't help emerging; indeed if we withheld our views there would be no point in writing this sort of book, but for us the aim remains open-ended. The reader will have his own views to draw upon, and his own experience of RE; he may have read other books in the field. Let him reach his own conclusions.

We have introduced a number of illustrations to show the sort of work which can be done on the blackboard. The requirements of the medium of pen and ink and of publication obviously mean that their present form is not quite the same as that which was seen by our pupils. But the basic planning and conception remain the same, and the reader will see that they are in essence still fairly uncomplicated and within the grasp of any averagely-talented teacher.

We gratefully acknowledge the help of a number of people: John Bowden at SCM Press who was prepared to risk this volume; Canon Angus Inglis of Nottingham who gave us a vision of excellence in our teacher training days; Gill Copley, for enduring our dramatic rehearsals in the lounge and then preparing the index, pausing only to make meals for the authors; the headmaster of Hinchingbrooke School, Huntingdon, for allowing us to use the school as the setting for chapters one and four, and especially for the support and encouragement he always gave to RE.

We ought to add that any supposition that there is any resemblance between the characters in this book and real people is
the result either of coincidence or of a guilty conscience. You are
quite at liberty to believe that the authors exist, though in this
scientific age the suspicion must remain that they are fictitious
names, like 'Ernie', intended to disguise the work of a computer or
committee.

The dedication of books – 'To Alice', 'To Pansy' etc. – is often
enigmatic. You may be wondering who the Hidden Man is. Actually
you already know him. He is part of a children's puzzle consist-
ing of all sorts of lines and shapes which don't make sense until
looked at in a certain way and from a certain angle. Then you can
see the outline of a man. Once you've seen him in the puzzle you
can always pick him out again straight away. The teacher's task,
whatever his subject, is to help the child to see the hidden man in
the subject puzzle.

Finally, in the preface most authors grovel in the dust before
the reader's feet and admit that the great things in a book are
owed to others, the mistakes to themselves. Not so for us. We each
claim credit for whatever is 'pleasing and of good report' and
blame the other for the rest.

Acknowledgments

We are grateful to the following for permission to quote from their works in this book:

The Editor, *Learning for Living*, for use of parts of the article by T. D. Copley 'Towards a New CSE Mode 1' in the issue of November 1973, here used in chapter 5; Longman Group Ltd for use of extracts from the book by Peter McPhail *In Other People's Shoes*, 1972, here used in chapter 7; the Schools Council and Hart-Davis Educational Ltd for the list of the aims and guidelines behind their RE Project material, here used in chapter 5; Arts et Métiers Graphiques, Paris, for permission to include copies of a wall carving first published by H. Bégouen and H. Breuil in *Les Cavernes du Volp*, 1958, here used on page 75; the Society of Antiquaries for permission to include a copy of a plan of one of the graves of Ur, first published by C. L. Woolley in the *Antiquaries Journal* VIII, 1928, here used on page 76; Miss Beverley McCallum of Hinchingbrooke School, Huntingdon, for use of part of her RE notebook, here used in Appendix III.

Another group of people helped us in actually giving birth to the manuscript: Mrs S. Blanchard, Mrs E. M. Fitzgerald, Miss J. Smith who typed out parts of the script in its early stages, risking their sanity in the process, and Messrs Wallis of York who prepared the final script; Messrs F. A. Fuge and K. Tonkin for helpful advice on artists' materials and techniques; Mr D. C. G. Fleming and Mr E. Martinez for help with the photography.

To all these people, and to any whose good ideas we have unwittingly plagiarized, we extend thanks.

1 Jake the Snake

It is nine o'clock on Monday morning. Lorries cough their fumes over the ring road as they encircle the town, *en route* north to the A1 or south to Cambridge and beyond. A lone green bus squats on the concrete area which locals call the bus station, waiting to depart to the London overspill estate. Huntingdon. In the factories and shops the week is beginning.

The schools also are starting their day with the usual 'act of worship'. We are concerned with one school, linear descendant of the grammar school attended by Cromwell and Pepys, heir to its tradition, now situated in spacious and pleasing grounds on the edge of town. How far has its school assembly changed over the years? Tiptoe into the back of the Lower School Hall, its serried rows of smart green uniforms; it is filled with a buzz of excitement from its young occupants. The stage curtains are closed. The hall vibrates to the thrilling grandeur of 'The Mastersingers' overture. A red-bearded member of staff stalks the stage.

'Stop talking now.' The buzz subsides.

'Oi, you there ... Didn't you hear what I said?' A pause.

'Right, stand.'

Two gowned figures stride rapidly between the rows of children down the hall and on to the stage. Excited whispers pass from mouth to mouth on either side. The two mount the stage and – to the intake of two hundred and forty breaths – one disappears straight through the closed curtains. The other turns, surveying the children with slight severity, and announces:

'Hymn number 142.' The piano strikes up. 'Mine eyes have seen the glory of the coming of the Lord' is sung with great vigour and feeling (if not understanding) by the children. Too soon, "While God is marching on' closes the final chorus and in a twinkling, while the children are still sitting down, the second gowned figure disappears into the wings. The curtains slowly open to reveal a table, two chairs, and on the table two glasses and a wine bottle.

Crawling surreptitiously on to the stage, back to the audience, is a tramp-like figure, clad in an old mac, and with a battered hat. He is obviously being furtive, but receives murmurs of acclaim from the audience – he is the first of the two gowned figures. He notices the murmur and turns, saying in a gutter-like voice:

'Oh, 'ello. Fancy seeing you in this 'ere restaurant. I thought it'd be empty. Well, I can't deny it. You've all 'eard o' me. My name's Jake the Snake (audience buzz). Yes, I'm the famous international criminal what is wanted in lots of countries for (he licks his lips and slowly enunciates) robbery with violence, violence without robbery and (he looks round hastily) stealing school custard (laughter).

'Even nah,' he continues, 'Chief Constable Ughes (Mr Hughes is head of the lower school) and 'is men is arter me. They is definitely arter me (renewed laughter).

'But I'm 'ere today on accahnt of me plan. I wouldn't be in this restaurant for the food; they do lousy dinners (applause). I'm 'ere (he looks conspiratorial) to do a big robbery. I am 'ere to rob the famous miser, Zachariah Scrimshaw (murmurs as they guess who will play the miser). This Scrimshaw's a nasty piece o' work. Ugly as sin. Mean as ... as ... as misery. But I gotta master plan. That's why this will be the perfect crime. In fact I'll let you have a look at it.' He puts a hand in his pocket and pulls out – a length of old blanket. He blows his nose on it and puts it away.

'It's 'ere somewhere ... the perfect plan. Maps, photos, diagrams, timing.' He continues to look, by now becoming agitated. He produces a half-eaten sandwich (laughter) and turns out his pockets one by one. It becomes clear that the plan is not there. He rushes about on the stage and down into the audience shouting:

'Don't panic. Don't panic. I've lost the plan for the perfect crime!' Appearing to calm down at last he returns slowly to the stage and continues:

'Never mind. Never mind. Even withaht a plan I'll rob 'im. I don't even know what he looks like (pause). All I can remember is that 'e's been tipped orff that I'm after 'im and 'e's in disguise as an RE teacher with a wooden leg (roars of laughter). Perhaps you'll 'elp me to rob 'im? (He appeals to the girls' half of the hall.) If you see him and I don't, give me a signal. (He pauses to think about this) ... I know, we'll 'ave a good, big wink. (He gives one – laughter.) Nah, we'll 'ave a re'earsal.' (The boys are very amused to see the girls' winking practice when Jake counts to three, and more so when the girls collapse giggling in an attempt to wink and Jake makes them try it again. But a sound is heard off, of wood beating on wood.)

'It could be 'im. That's 'is wooden leg. Nah remember (he winks at the girls) I'll get 'im withaht a plan (wooden noise again). Must hide.' Jake disappears off right.

On the left, however, singing begins. In dulcet tones and Oxford accent strains of 'Jerusalem the Golden' are heard. With slow, deliberate steps, Zachariah Scrimshaw enters. He too wears an overcoat, but a more prosperous one than Jake's. He wears a mortar board and carries a large black book marked 'Bible'. Coming to the table he takes out a small vanity mirror, props it on the bottle, and appearing not to notice the audience peers closely, turns from side to side, steps back and looks again, and says meditatively,

'Mmmmmm. *Looks* like an RE teacher. (Pause. Adjusts his mortar board.) *Dresses* like an RE teacher! (Audience titter – he walks up and down, backside noticeably protruding.) *Walks* like an RE teacher! (Audience laughter. He sniffs ...) *Smells* like an RE teacher! (hoots of laughter). By golly, it *is* an RE teacher!' Suddenly he is seized with convulsions of malevolent laughter and before the audience's astonished eyes he shrinks to his normal hunched and wizened posture. Removing his mortar board he sidles to the front of the stage and, glancing round, begins to speak – but not in the Oxford accent, rather in the accent of East London, with a Jewish flavour. He beckons to the audience.

'Psst!' Again he glances round. 'Psst! Moi noim ith Thcrimshaw. Thacariah Thcrimshaw, and oi'm dithgoithed ath an RE teacher.' He cackles softly, rubbing his knuckly hands. 'You want to know whoi oi'm in dithgoithe? Well, oi'll tell you for whoi. Oi'm after Joike the Thnoike! And oi'll tell you for whoi.' (Getting increasingly agitated he speaks louder and louder.) 'Oi'm after 'im 'cos 'e's after *moi money*!' Shocked by his indiscretion he claps his hand to his mouth and, wild-eyed, glances around him. He quickly changes tack. ... 'Monday, Tuesday, Wednesday. ...' (Audience groan.) 'Oi 'ave to look after moi money, you thee! That'th whoi oi keep it all in moi own pocket, where no one elthe can get hith hanth on it!' He pulls out a fat wad of bank notes (audience gasp), flicks through it lovingly and slaveringly, and replaces it carefully in his overcoat pocket. He takes out a mousetrap, sets it, and puts it in the same pocket.

'But oi'll have to be very careful, 'coth he'th been given a tip-off that oi'll be here. No, don't worry, everything'll be alroight, 'coth oi too 'ave been given a tip-off: yeth, *oi've* been given a tip-off that *he'th* been given a tip-off: that oi'll be here. So that'th whoi oi'm in dithgoithe! But (he looks morose) the trouble ith, oi've altho been given a tip-off that *he'th* been given a tip-off that *I've* been given a tip-off that *he'll* be here. So maybe he'll be in dithgoithe too!'

'Now that'th where you come in' (addressing the boys). 'Oi exthpect you've all theen 'im – an ugly piethe of work! (audience laughter). Hath a glath oiye! (more laughter). Now if you thee 'im, you tell me. You will tell me, won't you? (waits for boys' 'yes'). Oi'm a bit deaf; you'll 'ave to thay it louder! (boys shout *'yes'*). Good! Now we'd better arroinge a thecret thoign. Let'th thee. Oi know! If you thee 'im, you all thcratch your notheth. Loike thith (he demonstrates). We'll have a rehearsal. Now don't forget: you muthn't moike a noithe, it moit warn 'im. Roight now: one, two, three. . . .'

This time the girls have chance to laugh at the boys. Scrimshaw makes them repeat it until a vigorous and exaggerated scratching of the nose is achieved. But suddenly there is the sound of footsteps off. Scrimshaw freezes. Is there someone there? With slow, elaborate movement Jake enters on tiptoe but looking off. Scrimshaw has turned to look who is coming, but he is facing the wrong way to see Jake. Their backs touch. They stiffen. Each hunting the other, they tiptoe round full circle, still unaware that each is immediately behind the other. They turn simultaneously to face each other and say:

'How d'you do? . . . Aaaaaaaaargh!'

Each runs to his side of the audience asking 'Is it him?' Their reply constitutes the most vigorous display of winking and nose-scratching seen in the northern hemisphere. Affecting friendship, however, they smile and sit down together, removing their overcoats. Jake turns aside and says, 'Even withaht a plan I'll get 'im. Why (he gets up and wanders across to the edge of the stage), some people say a man withaht a plan's like a man withaht his trahsers, but I'll show 'em.'

While he is thus distracted, to the amazement of the audience Zachariah takes the wad of notes out of his own overcoat and, with ostentatious secrecy, places it in the pocket of Jake's coat. Jake remains unaware of these manoeuvres but, when they are over, returns to his seat, and they chat.

Z: Would you like to buy me a drink? (now resuming his Oxford accent, mortar board and Bible).

J: If you insist.

Z: Well, since you're paying, we'll have champagne.

J: Thank you (awkward pause).

Z: Funny people in this cafe (looks at the audience).

J: Yes.

Z: Look at the duffers at the back (howl of laughter as the school turn round to face the staff – red faces).

Champagne is brought to the table and Z stands up to pour the drink into the glasses, his back to J and the audience. J tiptoes out of his seat and, for everyone to see, hunts through Z's pockets. Z appears not to notice, even when J, amid howls of audience delight, is caught in the mousetrap. J also pulls out a large rubber spider.

J (to audience): It must be a money spider ... and this is obviously 'im. But where's the money? It must be 'ere somewhere. If only I 'ad me plan I wouldn't be in this mess.

Z (who has now finished pouring the champagne): Your glass! To health, wealth and happiness!

J: Yea! To health, *wealth*, and happiness! (Aside to audience:) I've solved it nah! I know where it is! It must be in 'is coat! But how can I get it? If only I 'ad me plan! (J moves to the table and picks up his own coat as if to leave.)

Z: Wait! Just a moment before you go. Have you never heard of the old Russian custom?

J: Eh? (surprised).

Z: When new friends drink a toast they always exchange coats.

J: (amazed and delighted that Z has himself suggested a plan which solves all J's problems, he rushes to the edge of the stage and excitedly tells the girls) I got 'im! I got 'im! (returns to Z, appearing to be doubtful). Change coats?

Z: Yes, come on, we've got to change coats now. (But his audience are beginning to realize what might happen.)

J (appearing to be persuaded): Well, if you insist. (They change coats. Cries of 'No', 'Don't', 'Stop', etc., from the audience do not dissuade Jake. Z goes out. Jake searches the new coat frantically. Finally, he pulls out a large sheet of paper and cries):

It's gotta be here. I've solved it!

But as he opens the sheet of paper no money is unveiled, only one word in large red lettering: SUCKER. Curtain.

J and Z take a bow, to loud applause. This time Jake remains and, discarding his coat and hat, turns to the audience, which is quelled by the appearance of his 'real' self and says simply:

'Some people go through life without a plan. They muddle from day to day, without ever asking what it's all about. Christians believe that God has a plan and it's up to us whether we want to be part of it or not.'

The bell rings for 9.30.

2 A Glass Eye for a Glass Eye

There must be as many reactions to the description in chapter 1 as there are people who read it. To some this may be a blasphemous travesty of what an assembly should be; to others a sugar-coated pill, with the bitter taste inevitably present; or an entertaining spectacle with a mini-moral tacked awkwardly on to the end.

Let the reader be quite clear that the authors – who presented the assembly described in chapter 1 – are their own severest critics. The challenge in the ending, for instance – how far does the plot really lead to this and to what extent is it an unhappy graft? We have come to the conclusion that difficulties inevitably arise out of the very nature of assemblies. How can large numbers of children with a variety of degrees of religious conviction from zero upwards 'worship' together in what Americans might call 'meaningful unity'? Yet the only way an assembly can succeed is by holding these two poles together. The ideal assembly is meaningful to all and its content is 'worshipful'.

How can this be achieved? Hymn-reading-prayer-punishment-notices-dismissal? The old recipe. It gives a fixed ritual start to every day, the comfortable security of the known. Preparation time is almost nil (Bible and prayer book open at well worn pages for this sort of assembly) and usage has sanctified the whole format. Presumably the assumption is a Christian society and a mini-church service. Those who endured seven years of secondary schooling with this sort of assembly will know that it left a lot to be desired.

What alternatives are there? The large number of assembly anthologies still published (and some are useful, e.g. *Words for Worship* by Campling and Davies or *Assembly Workshop* by R. Dingwall) shows that in many schools the ritual didn't change, only for the Bible was substituted some story of ethical or humanistic or Christian significance. Sometimes this worked quite well. James Thurber's fables, or Aesop's, or Colin Morris' *Thought for the*

Day (Radio 4) can provide thought-provoking material, and no one need, in our view, feel guilty about using these occasionally. But the form and the framework of such assemblies remained traditional.

Eventually some groups sought to replace the framework. The hymn was abolished; after all, some 75% of the audience/congregation were not Christians anyway, and some 75% of the 25% who were didn't understand the words, and of those remaining some were tone-deaf and couldn't sing it, some were shy and wouldn't, etc. The abolition of the hymn, however, removed one of the few pieces of audience involvement in the whole affair.

The prayer had to go, of course. It wasn't really 'on', it was said, to talk to God in a secular setting. So guided thought, or meditation, or just an embarrassed silence replaced it. Some secular topic such as pollution or poverty or war could then be tackled in a way which everyone could follow, whether they were atheist, Hindu or Christian. One was made to feel responsibility (sometimes guilt) about the topic of the day, though sometimes at the end one was left feeling rather impotent; after all, the children of Concrete City Comprehensive could hardly hope to remedy war or poverty.

Records were sometimes played to ginger up the proceedings. Often they confused the gathering, since the domestic record-player working full-tilt in a big hall is not easy to follow, with wow on the tweeter, woof on the flutter or whatever. A few enlightened souls duplicated the lyrics for the audience to follow, but this was rare (too much trouble).

Sometimes the secular assembly produced a monster of the most frightening dimensions – the moral homily. This was in fact a secular sermon, usually by one of the school hierarchy, on a topic such as litter. The point would be laboured, be-laboured and then go down fighting. The main weapon would be repetition and the Book of Revelation's sea of glass was often manifested in the faraway looks in the eyes of the children.

'Democratic' teachers began to enlist children to take assembly for them. 'They will give heed to their peers.' They did, if they could hear them, for very often their peers mumbled inaudibly at the front. Or they would persist in coming to ask you what to do, so that assembly often ended up with you taking it, via an intermediary, who gratefully delivered the material you had suggested. So some tried the Bible again, in the presentation of David Kossoff, Carl Burke *God is for Real, Man*, or others. The portcullis of indifference would still fall, however, at the mention of the word 'Bible'. The reaction against bibliolatry is far stronger among children than we imagine.

Then there is the subtle correlation between the attitude to assembly and the attitude to the school as a community by that community: its discipline, sense of purpose and so on somehow affect the tone of the assembly. Another background factor, often disregarded, is the physical environment of the assembly, crowded room, children standing, poor ventilation, etc. All this can destroy a promising assembly.

What can be concluded from all this? Chiefly that in practice one of our two aims – meaning and worship – has been lost. Some might say it was impossible to hold them together. We don't think the picture need look so black, but it does show that there is no panacea to the assembly problem, no set routine for success. There are guidelines, however, which can be laid down with a measure of confidence, and we list them here.

1. It is absolutely essential that the person or persons conducting the assembly should be clear what the aim is. This must be considered very carefully at the planning stage. Children resent being 'got at', whether by secular moral or Christian sermon, so it is desirable to present something thought-provoking which says 'Here's a view. Over to you,' rather than 'Thou shalt'.

2. There is some merit in making the finished product entertaining, or at least including some humour in the proceedings. At the very least the children may think that assembly can be fun. Then you do have their attention ready for the serious theme. And if at the end of it all the only thing they've derived from it has been the fun, then it's more than we derived in our childhood days. Serious does not equal dull, a principle we apply to RE as well as assembly.

3. Originality in assembly is worth striving for. This means longer preparation time, but the audience response shows that this is well worth the effort. Drama or dramatic monologues are always welcomed, provided they are not over-used. The dramatic monologues can be adapted to all levels of the secondary school, provided this is done sensitively. The slapstick type of presentation (as in chapter 1) in a sixth-form assembly must obviously give place to a more subtle, cerebral humour.

4. Variety in assemblies is also desirable. One man should not be identified with one type of assembly, e.g. drama; he should be seen to vary type and pace.

5. Some audience participation is essential. This may be in the informal way of the drama in chapter 1, or it may be a formal act such as a hymn, but we reject the reaction against 'trad' assemblies which renders the audience passive, because passivity leads to boredom and apathy.

6. Pupil participation in the running of assemblies is essential, though not necessarily as the norm. This really speaks for itself. However, children taking assembly need help on the mechanics from staff, guidance on voice-projection, etc. Seldom tried is the concept of children and staff sharing the leadership. This seems to us a valuable step forward. Some schools have assembly committees to arrange the rota for the term and plan any special assemblies; these committees usually consist of staff and students and can serve a very useful function, especially in a large school where, say, they can approach the head of lower school to take sixth-form assembly on a given day. The committee can often provide a greater variety of speakers and leaders than one harassed member of staff frantically scratching up a rota is able to do.

7. Assemblies should never be run and controlled by the RE department. The aim and ethos of assembly is not the same as that of RE. However modern an assembly is, it simply is not a mass RE lesson for two hundred or more children. The aims of assembly are still, in some sense, hortatory or didactic. The aims of RE are discussed more fully later. Suffice it here to say that RE should be open-ended, and the student as an individual must play a larger part than in assembly. It can be harmful to RE if pupils identify the aims of RE and assemblies; RE teachers should not be seen as vicar figures. At the same time, it is probably equally undesirable to dissociate the RE department from assemblies altogether. The RE staff, like all other staff, should be prepared to take their share. A thorough grounding of hard work is needed to back a successful assembly, coupled with enthusiasm and – in our case – a background of rivalry.

'Let's kill Mr Copley by Voodoo' is a suggestion eagerly assented to by Mr Easton's class and a plasticine doll can soon be made. A class discussion on where to stick the first pin. Leg? Arm? Stomach? Arm it is, and all breaths are held as the pin is lovingly inserted into the doll. Emissaries are speedily dispatched to Mr Copley's lesson on the pretext of borrowing chalk. They return elated. He was holding his arm as if in pain while teaching! The course on primitive religion takes on a new significance for the class. But wait! A knock at the door. It is Mr Copley who says in low tones to his colleague (naturally all the children listen intently),

'I've just come to see if you can spare a text book for first year work. I'm one short.' His colleague obliges.

'Do you know,' continues the visitor, 'I've started with a pain in my arm; rheumatism, I suppose.' The class is silent and mystified. Mr Copley turns to go. Quickly the pin is pulled out of the doll, unseen by him, but he turns. 'Well, that's a funny thing,' he says, 'that pain's gone, just as suddenly as it came.' Murmurs through the class, until one bright spark cries out 'He's having us on.'

After indignant denials and further insistence from the class the plot is confessed. It was all rigged. Mr Easton 'guided' the decision to prick the doll's arm. A hoax. All is well. Mr Copley leaves, avowing that he will trip up Mr Easton's wooden leg. The latter returns that he wouldn't be at all surprised – if Mr Copley's glass eye is looking, one can only expect clumsiness.

Weeks later Mr Copley is teaching a class about the hiding of certain Christians from Nazi interrogators, and to make their escape more realistic sneaks out of the classroom himself. Suddenly the door is flung open and in strides Herr Easton in 'SS' mackintosh, with suitable hat and glasses. He harangues the astonished class with a strong German accent to try to discover the fugitive and concludes: 'Ve haf vays of mekink you talk.' Then he disappears into the corridor. His colleague can now return and continue the drama with 'Has he gone?'

How was this rigged? Simply by careful planning and the coincidence of Mr Easton having a 'free' period when his colleague intended to teach the topic.

Or again, a class of twelve-year-olds might suddenly find the wrong RE teacher coming in to take their lesson. He appears not to notice that he is in the wrong class and astonishes them by teaching the lesson as if he took them every time. He even begins by saying,

'Now last time just as the bell went we were talking about—— and Richard answered a question on ——.' A use of the same technique outlined above.

Then again there are the scurrilous stories, of how one's colleague escaped from Hitler disguised as a tomato, a bowl of fruit, etc. There is listening for wooden footsteps, a Christmas collection for a tin of furniture polish for the wooden leg, and careful staring to try to establish which is the glass eye (and children are not being encouraged to laugh at real-life deformities – they realize that the fun lies in there being no 'real-life' glass eye or wooden leg in this case). To relate that one is seventy-six years old and should be retired, except that the Prime Minister phoned the other night and begged one to carry on, in order that one's colleague should not take over, meets with acclaim. A chance encounter of Copley and Easton in the lower school corridor with swarms of partisan children around provides an opportunity that is too good to miss. A collision at the staff-room door leads to: 'Want to make a fight of it?' They step into the staff-room. Yells, buffets, thuds are heard outside, but nothing is seen by the pupils because the windows are of frosted glass. Then the two combatants emerge, considerably dishevelled, and with sticking plaster on their faces. The requirements? Spontaneity, an impromptu use of available props, in this case a tin of plasters, and a spirited pugilistic yell. This yell has the interesting effect of alerting any one who has slumbered for years beneath *The Times* in the staff-room.

And of course eleven- and twelve-year-old children are entertained, excited and puzzled by all these antics; they eagerly look forward to the next round and 'champion' their RE teacher vigorously. Each lesson starts in an atmosphere of suppressed excitement. But the question must arise as to how all this larking about can possibly qualify as education. The answer is perfectly simple: it doesn't even claim to. It is merely the framework within which we teach, just as in many subjects there can be a framework of dull conventionality. It can, however, justifiably claim to break the primary school boredom or the child's expectation of secondary schooling, with a dynamic impact. Enthusiasm is contagious. To connect RE with liveliness and (we hope) excellence, to make our eleven- and twelve-year-olds long for the RE lesson, creates a lasting impression and removes the possibility of an anti-RE barrier higher up the school.

Our post-primary child needs surprise, fantasy, humour, excitement as well as academic instruction and the development of skills. We try to cater for the 'whole child'. One might add the interest and amusement/appreciation/mystification felt by parents and expressed at parents' evenings. They too can enjoy the backwash of all this.

Obviously combined with this is the humour, discipline, entertainment and hard graft of the subject teaching with class/group/individual work. Otherwise RE would be just a laugh. But we feel that often an undue emphasis on 'projects' (which have been endured through the long primary years), an over-use of the group work method at a stage when the child wants to express himself as an individual more, can deprive the child of this chance to meet the teacher, not only as group supervisor, but as (dare one say it?) class teacher and performer. The subject's image does matter. Children need to be shocked out of their inherited assumption that religious study is dull. They must not be allowed to cherish the illusion that you are sent by the establishment to pump religion into them. They must not be allowed to think of RE as the Cinderella subject, crowded into a tiny corner on the timetable. The only possible answer is impact – which for us takes the form described in these chapters. As the American gangster put it, 'You guys gotta think big.'

3 The Case of the Sneezing Teacher

Holmes was never, I fear, a man much interested in matters of religion. Whether this was due to the presence of some deeply-lying and ineradicable distemper, or merely to the clamour of the multitudinous tasks with which he was so incessantly encumbered, I cannot say. It is indeed possible that this singular short-coming may have been the product of the many years he had spent in pursuit of scientific knowledge. Whatever the cause, it is certain that during the entire course of our association Holmes never showed the slightest disposition to discuss with me any aspect of the supernatural.

Yet there was a period when, for a short while, I found myself seriously questioning whether Holmes might not be taking an unusual interest in this very field. For he appeared at this time to be probing into occult practices of the most devilish and villainous kind. It had, as I recall, been an unusually cold spring, and Holmes had had little to occupy him for some weeks. As was generally his way at such times, he had taken to fitful experimentation at his table of chemicals and to long hours on the violin. I availed myself meanwhile of the opportunity to read some medical journals which had accumulated over the past year. I was reading just such a journal one morning in late March when Holmes suddenly put down his violin.

'A charming piece, don't you think?'

'Eh, what's that?' I said, looking up from my book.

'My dear Watson, I'm sorry, I really shouldn't have interrupted your reading.'

'Not at all, Holmes; not at all. It was not an article of any great consequence.'

'I was merely commenting on the charming character of the last piece I played: one of the lesser-known works of Albinoni, the Fantasy in D. I have myself recently prepared a critical edition of the work.'

'You never cease to amaze me, Holmes.'

'A somewhat unflattering compliment, but predictable nonetheless.' Holmes strolled to the window and stood gazing down into the street.

'Quick Watson!' he suddenly exclaimed. 'Bring me my binoculars! Hurry, man!'

'Whatever is the matter, Holmes? I hope nothing is amiss.'

'No, there is nothing amiss; at least not with us. But I fancy we shall shortly be receiving a visit from an RE teacher from Crampton for whom, to judge from his appearance, there is something very much amiss. Things are looking up, my friend.'

'Good gracious, Holmes! You never cease to . . .' At that moment there came a ring at the doorbell.

'Ah, this should be our man. Show up our RE teacher would you please, Watson?'

I opened the front door to find myself face to face with a man of undistinguished appearance. His build was neither excessively heavy nor excessively light; but his face, sallow and haggard, revealed the incisions of increasing age and deep anxiety. He paused, breathless, on the doorstep.

'Mr Sherlock Holmes?'

'My name is Watson; Dr Watson. You will find Mr Holmes upstairs.'

'Thank heaven!' exclaimed the visitor, and after a moment's hesitation made his way agitatedly up the stairs. He was greeted at the top by Holmes.

'Good morning. I presume it is me you have come to see?'

'Mr Holmes? Allow me to introduce myself: Cyril Windrush.'

'How do you do? Won't you come through into the study?'

'Thank you.'

'You have made very good time coming from Crampton; though I am sorry you had to run to catch the train.'

The stranger fell back aghast, his haunted eyes wide with astonishment. I must confess that I too was surprised in no small measure.

'How on earth do you know I come from Crampton?'

'A simple matter of deduction; it's quite elementary. But as I perceive you have been at pains to hasten your arrival here, I presume that you have called on a matter of some urgency. If you will be so good as to take a seat, then you can tell me the nature of your business, starting from the beginning, if you please. You may speak freely before my colleague, Dr Watson; he assists me in all my investigations.'

The visitor collapsed into an armchair facing Holmes and began to recount his strange tale.

'As you know, I come from Crampton. I am a teacher by profession.'

'An RE teacher; please be precise.'

'But how do you know?'

'Never mind about that. Pray proceed.'

'Well, then, it is true. I am an RE teacher by profession and I work at Crampton Comprehensive. As you can see, I am no longer in my prime; but in normal circumstances I could expect to be teaching for another ten or fifteen years. I have always enjoyed my work. I find it a congenial way of life and after my first few years I soon learned to teach without undue effort or expenditure of energy. In time I gained promotion to be head of my own department, a post which I have, I think, held with reasonable competence. At first there were a number of adjustments to be made to the syllabus and methods of the department; but once I had put our work on a sound biblical basis I found that my new job was relatively undemanding, there being little but the normal routine work to do. And so, for the last fifteen or twenty years I can honestly say that in my work I have been free of worries. And, as I said, I could have expected this state of affairs to continue until my retirement. That was until the Thursday before last, just over a week ago.'

'Ah! Now we come to it!' murmured Holmes, leaning keenly forward.

'Mr Holmes, I am an equable man by nature, not much given to panic or fear. But it is no exaggeration to say that since that Thursday the whole of my teaching career has fallen into tatters. The whole foundation of my work has been knocked away. I can no longer sleep, I am confused; my confidence is so shattered that I scarcely dare face a class. This alone is bad enough, for if it continues my whole career will be in jeopardy. But in addition to this, Mr Holmes, I must tell you that I have been haunted by the most terrible fears. Fear of ... of ...'

'Yes?'

Leaning forward he lowered his voice to barely a whisper. 'It is fear of ... the visions.'

'Visions? So there have been more than one?'

'Oh yes, indeed. Regularly every day, and always at school. And they always happen in exactly the same way. Each morning at nine o'clock we call the register in our classrooms, and then the school goes into the hall for assembly. This normally lasts until nearly 9.25. When it is over, the staff leaves the hall first, myself included. I generally go straight to my room to make whatever last-minute preparations are necessary before my pupils come in for the first lesson. This means that I am on my own in the room for perhaps five minutes. It is in this period for the last six mornings at school that ... that I have seen them. I go into my room, start to tidy the books on my desk and then, with no warning, the whole room begins to billow full of coloured fumes; and then ... then one of them appears. A different one each day, each more terrible than the last. I tremble to think of it.'

'Perhaps it would help you to talk about it. Tell me about the first of these, er, visions.'

'It began like all the others, as I was later to discover. First came the clouds, and then, to my horror, I saw in the middle of the room an enormous man dressed in bishop's robes. He was old and severe, with deep wrinkles and a long grey beard. His penetrating gaze chilled me to the marrow. And then he spoke ...

'I am Papias. Who has summoned me?'

'You're wh ... wh ... who?'

With a howl of rage the apparition cast back its shaggy head and, shaking its crook in the face of heaven, roared,

'Is it for this miserable ignoramus that I have been brought all the way from the second century?' Then, 'You, boy! Where did you learn your theology that you have never heard of Papias?'

'P .. p .. please, Mr Papias ...' The apparition raised its hoary brows and slowly shook its mitred head from side to side, the while fixing me with its gaze.

'I mean, sir ... headmaster ... my lord ...' The apparition became still.

'I'm afraid, my lord, that I n .. n .. n .. never really d .. did any theology.'

'No theology?' growled the figure.

'At least, not in a college or anything ... though of course I read plenty of religious paperbacks. You see, I'm really an engineer ...'

'And how, pray, can an engineer teach Religious Education?'

'Well, sir ... my lord ... I usually simply teach the Bible. The life of Christ, for example; based on St Mark.'

'Ahh?'

'Er .. er .. er ..'

'Ahhhhh?'

'Er...We-start-off-with-the-birth-stories-of-course-from-Matthew-
and-Luke-and-then-go-through-the-three-years-of-Jesus'-ministry-in
-chronological-order-following-St Mark-it's-the-earliest-gospel-so-it's
-probably...'

'Just as I thought! You miserable worm, teaching the life of
Christ in so-called chronological order! Now if you had done some
theology,' he said, pointing a quivering finger, 'you would know
what every scholar has known since I wrote in the second century.'

'W .. w .. what's that?'

'That Mark wrote down the stories of Peter, but *not, however,
in order*!'

'But, but, how shall I teach, then?'

'You expect *me* to tell *you* how to teach?'

'No .. er .. yes .. that is, who can I ask?'

'Oh, I expect we will be able to arrange some tuition for you.
Another vision perhaps! Yuk, yuk, snigger, snigger.'

... And wagging his beard with a mirthful clicking of brown
and yellow teeth, cheshire-cat-wise, he gradually vanished.

'Well, Mr Holmes, you can imagine how shaken I was. You
see, I had never seen a vision before. And besides that, so much
of my teaching was being called into question. I was thoroughly
confused. But I thought that this vision was no more than an
isolated event, and prepared to put it out of my mind. But then the
next morning, the Friday, the same thing happened again.'

'The same figure?'

'No, different this time. A large man, wreathed in cigar-smoke,
with a lined face and small grey moustache. He was stooping over
a lecture-desk ...'

'Goot mornink. Ich bin Professor Bultmann. Der subject of
dis mornink's lecture iss an outline of de results of tventieth
century New Testament scholarship, mit special reference zu der
four gospels. Jawohl!

'It iss now apparent zat ve can no lonker regard de gospels as
simple biographies of Jesus. For some years ve heff been studying
in grossester detail de precise forms taken by der individual stories
und sayinks vich ve find in de gospels, und ve heff learned to
trace somezink of de process by vich each of dese stories – or

pericopae, as ve call dem – came to be written down. Ve now know better zan ever before, dat vot ve heff in de gospels iss not ein collection of eyevitness reports, but ein treasury of de early church's communal memories of Jesus.

'Der recognition zat dese pericopae circulated in der early church as individual stories, passed on from mouth to mouth for some time before they were collected und written down – zis recognition has ein important corollary. It iss dat in many cases der original context of der story hass been lost. But careful scholarship iss helping us to rediscover dese lost settings. Sometimes, indeed, ve find zat dey differ from a setting given in one or even perhaps several, of de gospels. An evaluation of de newly discovered contexts is permitting ein neues picture of Jesus to emerge – a picture of ein very controversial und outgespoken figure.

'Ve can also now appreciate more clearly vot de writers of de gospels vished to convey, for ve can assume zat zey selected und arranged de pericopae according to zeir own particular designs.

'Der study of de gospels, zerefore, hass not still gestood, und great advances heff been made. It vill be found zat zey heff considerable implications for der teaching of religion at all levels. Danke schön. Zat concludes dis mornink's lecture. Auf Wiedersehen, und Heil Formgeschichte!'

The elderly professor turned as if to leave.

'But Professor Bultmann!'

'Ja?'

'But Professor, it's all very well your barging in here and saying all that. But I've got children to teach. How am I going to teach them the gospels if you say that so much of them is unreliable?'

'Vell now, zat issn't quite vot I said. But still, you vant to teach der children about Jesus, ja? I heffn't vorked out ein syllabus myself, but as it so heppens, I heff heard of one vich is based on such results of modern scholarship. It attempts to set der life of Christ vithin der context of ein study of der early church – vich itself is put into der context of der church today. So der life of Christ iss presented as vot der early church remembered about Jesus; und it is not studied as ein biography or as ein history, but simply by der major themes by vich der early church itself remembered Jesus. In zis way der gospel material is presented in accordance mit der true nature of de sources. You will also remark zat der whole subject is set within a vider sphere, as part of ein study of religions of faith. Der study of der church iss followed mit einem introduction zu some other religions. Diss all follows der pattern laid down in der first form.

'Ach, but of course you heff not yet seen der Firstformsyllabus! In zat case at any rate you can make a start through studying dis one. Here iss ein copy: ist intended to be ein Secondformsyllabus. I will leave you to study it. Guten Morgen.'

And he disappeared into the cigar-smoke.

'Have you the paper with you?' asked Holmes. 'Ah, thank you. Hmm. Most revealing.'

The paper read as follows:

FORM II SYLLABUS

'RELIGIONS OF FAITH'

I. CHRISTIANITY

1. *The church today*

(a) Start with what the children, inevitably, know about the church – 'churches'. Why do they look different from most other buildings? Historical, functional, aesthetic, devotional reasons, e.g. altar rails to keep the dogs out, towers and spires having 'public relations' value, windows for education.

Opportunities for slides, displays; projects on monastery and abbey remains.

(b) But are religious buildings necessary to religion? This turns the tables on the pupils and has some shock value. The Jerusalem temple as a notable example; origins under David and Solomon, a tool of self-aggrandisement, the catastrophic results. Jeremiah's criticisms.

(c) Then what is the church really? Not buildings but people. What does the church do (apart from holding services)? Caring for people. William Booth and the Salvation Army as an example. Opportunity also for study of other explicitly Christian charities. But why is there a church at all? This leads back to ...

2. *The early church*

(a) Pentecost: the beginning of the church's self-awareness.

(b) What was the early church like? How does it compare with today's church? Points of characteristic difference: no buildings, common life, the prominence of healing and preaching. Examples such as Ananias and Sapphira (if you can brave it!), the man at the Beautiful Gate, Stephen's preaching (which also picks up the theme of the temple again), Stephen's 'trial' and death. This leads into ...

(c) A conspectus of the life of one prominent preacher in the early church: Paul, the travelling preacher. His conversion. His background. His belief – Christianity for all men (Council of Jerusalem). Favourable conditions in the ancient world – universal language, safe travel, religious enquiry. Paul's advantages – education, Roman citizenship.

Paul's travels – a selection. Emphatically not an exhaustive study of Paul's journeys. Notable incidents at Philippi, Ephesus and Athens. This last highlights the importance of Jesus' resurrection in Paul's preaching.

Paul as a letter-writer and teacher.

Briefly, the Jews' revenge and Paul's fate. This is simply for the sake of completeness and should not occupy more than a lesson or two.

But where did Paul learn his belief in the first place?

(d) What the early church remembered about Jesus – the teaching of the early church. Jesus' resurrection – examine simply some of the problems here, and discuss why the early Christians thought it was important. This raises the problem of sources. The gospels: why they were written when they were – eyewitnesses dying out, persecution situation etc. What the gospels are based on – oral tradition; why there is more than one gospel and why there are differences. With especially bright classes a brief look at the synoptic problem can be included.

What was remembered about Jesus' life? Fact and fiction in the story of Jesus' birth. And then a study of themes – teaching, healing, opposition, death.

Teaching: especially by parables. Examples, preferably using lesser-known parables. Establish first, by close questioning, that the pupils all think they understand some of the well-known parables but that in fact they don't understand them at all. Hence the need to look at them again, despite previously massacred versions in Sunday school and junior school. The unjust judge, the friend at midnight, the ten bridesmaids, the great supper. No moralizing!

Healings: as a method of teaching (the nature of faith). Some examples – e.g. the Gerasene demoniac, Jairus' daughter, the paralytic. With especially bright classes one may attempt an elementary study of principles of interpretation – viz. the 'literalist' approach, the 'rationalist' approach and the 'symbolist' approach.

Opposition to Jesus: the reasons for it – association with tax collectors. Why tax collectors were unpopular. Matthew. Zacchaeus. Sabbath-breaking: the sabbath in the Pharisaic tradition. The cornfields incident. The man with the withered hand. Insults to the religious leaders. The cleansing of the temple. Jesus as a controversial figure, *not* 'meek and mild'. Culmination: Judas and his motives, the arrest, the trials, and the death.

3. *Tradition in the church*
How the early church's memories got passed on to us.

(*a*) The passing down of the gospels. Eye-witnesses, oral tradition, evangelists, manuscripts, scribes and monks, translations, printing. Brighter children always get surprisingly interested in manuscript problems – how variants arise, how the text can be restored. Reference can be made to the enchanting story of Tischendorf and the Codex Sinaiticus.

(*b*) The monks who passed on the gospels. As history departments seem to be obsessed with teaching 'the life of the mediaeval monk', this aspect of the topic is best by-passed in RE. Concentrate instead on the monastic ideal, perhaps presented as a protest movement. Antony, Simeon Stylites, Benedict, Francis.

(*c*) The gospels passed on to the church today in modern translations. Opportunity for comparison and expression of preferences. This brings us back, full circle, to the church today.

II. OTHER RELIGIONS OF FAITH (AN INTRODUCTION)

1. *Islam*
(*a*) Mohammed: his call in the desert, Mecca and the condition of religion there. His message for Mecca. His career as a ruler. Holy war. The spread of Islam.

(*b*) Moslem beliefs: Allah, the Koran, idolatry.

(*c*) Religious practices: mosques, pilgrimage, prayer, the Kaaba, art.

2. *Buddhism*
(*a*) Siddharta Gautama, the Buddha: events before his birth – his mother's dream and its significance. The consequences: his enclosed early life, seeing the signs. His decision to become a monk, and his disillusionment. The Bo-tree and enlightenment.

(*b*) Buddhist teachings, simply (!): the middle way, nirvana.

(*c*) Buddhist practices: meditation, monks, temples.

3. *Hinduism*
    (*a*) The absence of a founder.
    (*b*) Hindu life and religious practices: the importance of water, reincarnation, the caste system, vegetarianism.

NOTE: One would expect this syllabus to occupy roughly the following time scale:
    Term I: I, 1 and 2 (*a*), (*b*), (*c*).
    Term II: I, 2 (*d*) – 3 (*c*).
    Term III: II, plus exams.

'I take it you have read this?'

'Indeed I have, Mr Holmes. And I may say that I was nothing short of horrified. You could never base lessons of bible-reading on this. It would be far too confusing for the children, jumping as it does from place to place in the gospels. The one consolation is that at least you can teach the parables in the old way. That has not been upset. At least, I'm not sure now. I thought that at first, but then on Monday there came a third vision, this time of two men, sitting in armchairs and drinking tea ...

'Won't you have another cream puff, Professor Jeremias?'

'Thank you, no. I had much Wurst on the aeroplane. It was not very good. In fact it was the worst I have had for years. But I must say that it is a wonderful thing that you and I have at last met, Professor Dodd. So now we can have a good chat about parables, ja?'

'Not before time, either, considering that your book and mine are the best general works on the subject.'

'Ja, that is right, ha! ha!'

'Well, it seems that we are agreed on the basic principles. We broadly agree with Bultmann that if the parables are to be properly understood, we have to work out carefully how Jesus originally used them.'

'Ja, and also the ways in which they may have been adapted during the period of oral transmission.'

'Well, you have looked at that more than I have. But, you know, there's one crucial question we have not said anything about in our books – at least, not explicitly. That is, how would we recommend school teachers to deal with the parables? What are your ideas on the matter?'

'Vell now. I think first of all they should always try to show

how Jesus used parables. They were arguments, not sermons.
When people criticized him, he replied with a parable.'

'Yes, I quite agree. So that means they should always be put
into context. And they certainly shouldn't be treated as moral
sermons. It makes me shudder to think of the way they are sometimes used in assemblies.'

'It is so. But one of the difficulties with parables is to bring them
to life. The trouble is that in the gospels a lot of background
information is taken for granted which modern readers no longer
always know about.'

'Which example had you in mind?'

'Take the parable of the great supper, for instance. The first half
of the story doesn't appear in the Bible at all. It vos so common
in those days that everyone knew it. What Jesus did was to add
a surprise ending to a vell-known folk tale. So if a teacher is going
to tell this parable, I think he ought to start right at the very
beginning with the bit that you can't read in the gospels. So he
should tell his class about the snobbish, self-satisfied, wealthy
village into which, to everyone's disgust, there moves in one day
a tax collector. How can he, of all people, afford to move into a
village like this? On a salary like his? There's something funny
going on somewhere. Besides, who wants to have anything to do
with a tax collector? So the villagers carefully ignore the new-
comer. But the tax collector is determined to make an impression.
He's one of the upper class now. So he vorks out a plan. He vill
give the most lavish dinner the villagers ever saw ... And so the
parable begins.'

'Yes; but the problem with that is that the teacher has to have
some knowledge of extra-biblical sources. And he needs to know
what he's talking about. The parables aren't as simple as they
look.'

'Just let them try to work out the precise significance of the seed
in the parable of the sower!'

'Ho! Ho! Ho!'

'Ho! Ho! Ho!'

The vision faded.

'You will appreciate, Mr Holmes; this was the last straw. Of
all my teaching methods, nothing was left – nothing. I couldn't
teach the life of Christ, we couldn't read the Bible, I couldn't even
teach the parables. Whatever I did, some vision told me to do it
differently. I was at my wits' end. And on top of all this, I have

been losing hours of sleep every night worrying over the parable of
the sower. What am I to do, Mr Holmes? Tell me, what am I to
do?'

'Perhaps I could refer you to my own recent monograph on the
subject. An excellent book. I can recommend it.'

'Aaaghghugh!' (convulsions).

'Well another time, perhaps. I think you said that the vision of
Dodd and Jeremias occurred on Monday, did you not? Yet it is
now Thursday. You've been a long time mentioning the matter.'

'But, you see, each day I hoped and prayed that I had seen the
last of the visions. Only now do I know that I can expect another
tomorrow. That is why I am seeking your help now.'

'So there have been more visions since Monday?'

'Alack, yes!' exclaimed the miserable Windrush, wringing his
hands in desperation. 'Every day!'

'Well I must hear about them. In order, if you please.'

Windrush heaved a deep sigh, and then resumed his melancholy
tale.

'Tuesday's vision was especially strange, Mr Holmes. For it was
heralded not just by coloured fumes, but by coloured lights, and
fairground music, and the sound of a voice, crying ...

'Is it a bird? Is it a plane? It's ...

WIGLEY!'

'Spare me!'

'Ah! I see we have a poor, frustrated RE teacher on our hands!
Now then, what seems to be the matter? Take your time and tell
Uncle Wigley all about it.'

'Oh, Uncle Wigley ... (sniff!) ... I've been having such a terrible
time. All these nasty bishops and professors have been getting at
me – Papias and Bultmann and Jeremias and Dodd and ... (sniff!)

... I'm all confused and ... (sniff!) ... they're telling me to teach the gospels in funny ways I don't understand, and ... (sniff!) ... and ... (sniff!) ... I'm only an ordinary RE teacher, and ... (sniff, sniff!) ... and ... (sniff!) ...'

'There, there, Cyril; don't worry your little head about all that. It will all come if you give it calm study and a bit of thought. Anyway, you weren't going to teach the gospels to this year's first form, were you? It's much better to let it wait till the second form. So you see, you have till next year to work it out.'

'Yes ... (gulp) ... I suppose you're right. Well, perhaps this year won't be so bad after all. I'll carry on with the Old Testament in Form I. We've got as far as II Kings.'

'Oh ... Oh, dear me.'

'Oh, no! Don't tell me you're going to start too now, are you, Uncle Wigley?'

'Well I must say I don't like the sound of that Form I syllabus very much. Is that what you always do?'

'Yes' (petulantly) 'and it's been a very good system up till now. The Old Testament in Form I, the gospels in Form II, and Acts in Form III.'

'Oh dear, oh dear! Now I can see why they've been getting at you. Now suppose we try to work out something positive? What about starting off your new first-formers with something that has a bit of impact? What do you do for your first lesson?'

'Er ... (sniff) ... let me see. I think we do a map of the fertile crescent.'

'Well, that hasn't got much impact, has it? What you want is something that's really going to get your new pupils keen and excited. You must get them thinking that RE is the best subject on the whole timetable.'

'I don't know if I can.'

'Nonsense, of course you can. All you need is a first-rate syllabus, some good methods, and plenty of enthusiasm. I'll send someone else to tell you about the methods, but here's an idea for the syllabus: why not do some work on primitive religion?'

'Primitive religion???!! How's that supposed to benefit my pupils, I'd like to know?'

'It would widen their horizons, for a start. Your pupils would begin to think about the fundamental question, "What is religion?" And if you included topics such as ancient ideas on how the world began, then you would be putting over the concept of myth at a commendably early age. That would help you avoid all the difficulties you usually get later over the question of science and religion.'

'But I don't see how you would organize it all, or where you could get all the information from.'

'Perhaps my text book would help? It's called *From Fear to Faith*. It sets out a history of early religion, by themes such as "middlemen", "sacrifice", "the family", "death", and shows how religion progressed from being based on fear to being based on faith. It has some very exciting material in it, though I say so myself.'

'So the Old Testament has to go as well, then?'

'In the way you're using it at present, yes. But a lot of Old Testament stories are very good illustrations for a history of early religion. So you can still use it, but with more discretion and together with other material of a similar type from a wider background. Let me give you a couple of examples.

'A good story in the Old Testament is the story of Abraham and Isaac. But is there really any educational value in just teaching it as a story in its own right? It just becomes a fairy tale. But supposing you are teaching about sacrifice in early religion. Then the story illustrates beautifully one of the key steps that was made in the progression from fear to faith – the step from giving human sacrifices to giving only animal sacrifices. As a matter of fact, that is probably the significance the early Jews saw in the story in the centuries before it was put down in writing in its present position in Genesis.

'We could take another example from Genesis, too. I expect you teach your pupils the story of the creation of the world in six days, from Genesis 1? Yes, I thought you might. And do you also tell them the different creation story in Genesis 2? I thought not. Well, you should. Then they would realize that these stories should not be taken literally. And while you're about it, it's a good idea to include some of the comparable, but different, Mesopotamian and Egyptian ideas. If you do it carefully, the distinctive implications of each can be made to stand out – how the Egyptians thought the world got here by accident and the Jews thought it was by God's design.'

'But I can't cope with all that sort of thing!'

'You've got a theological training, haven't you? ... Oh! I see – yes, well there could be problems then. But still, time and hard work will rectify that. It's really worth making the effort, you know, Cyril. I bet most of your pupils come here thinking that RE will

be just the same as it was at Sunday school and primary school –
the same old Bible stories being ground out over and over again.
And they're right, aren't they? No wonder RE is at the bottom of
the charts. Now if you tried this scheme – well, it would really
liven things up. Here, let me give you a syllabus. ... Yes, I know
you've just had one from Professor Bultmann recently, but that
one is best used with Form II. This is for Form I. It's not mine
actually, but it is largely based on my book. There now, dry your
eyes and blow your nose; you've got a class waiting outside ...'

'And here it is, Mr Holmes. This is what he gave me.'

FORM I SYLLABUS

WHAT IS RELIGION?

The story of religion is a story of development from fear to
faith.

1. *Fear*

The dominating characteristic of early religion. What early man
was afraid of, and why. How this led to a form of religion: fetishes,
ancestor worship, belief in magic, belief in ghosts, voodoo, witchcraft. 'Primitive' religion still exists: lucky charms, local ghost
stories, modern witchcraft.

2. *Ideas about gods*

How they developed from fear to faith: animism, nature gods,
and the fear of their failure; Marduk and Tiamat (the battle between
good and evil), compare Mazda and Ahriman etc.; Egyptian sun
worship; ancient gods we still remember in commercial and other
contexts (e.g. Mazda, Mars, Apollo, Vesta, etc., etc.). Cars, fashion,
drink money – are those modern 'gods'? Some people behave as
though they were. The development of the idea of God: Moses
and 'I am' (monotheism); Elijah on Mt Horeb (God speaking in
the mind); the Christian idea of God (caring for men).

3. *Why is the world here?*

Answers of fear and faith to this central question of religion.
Egyptian ideas, especially Ra's sneeze: the world got here by
accident. Babylonian ideas, especially Marduk's destruction of
Tiamat: the world got here because of a fight. The two Jewish
ideas in Genesis: the world is here because God wants it to be.
This whole section is probably best presented pictorially. The

concept of myth can be introduced. The section has ancillary importance as a corrective for notions of biblical inerrancy, often picked up in Sunday school and junior school.

4. *Middlemen*

Their early emergence in religion, often as objects of fear, but also as providers, advisers, healers, intercessors. Witch doctors, the Shaman: what they really do, and why they are held in awe; rainmaking in Africa and in ancient Chinese and Japanese religions; witch doctors and their methods of healing. The witch doctor as a psychiatrist.

Seers – what they saw and how (e.g. hepatoscopy, sacred chickens etc.); omens; oracles – Oedipus and the oracle of Delphi; dreams – their importance ancient and modern, the story of Joseph; 'primitive' types of middleman still survive – fortune tellers, horoscopes, palmistry: how do they work? Do they tell the truth?

The development of middlemen. Elijah and the contest on Mt Carmel: rainmaking linked with belief in one God. Elisha and Naaman: healing linked in the same way. The rise of priests, with duties, uniforms (ancient and modern) and place of work. This leads on to ...

5. *Sacrifice*

Early sacrifice as giving the best, often out of fear. Examples from e.g. Eskimos, Maya Indians, Pawnee Indians, Pacific Islanders. Early man's fear of being without rain and food: sacrifices to Sedna, Moloch, Tlaloc. Human sacrifice in various early religions, especially Aztec.

The development of the idea of sacrifice. Abraham and Isaac: animal sacrifice instead of human sacrifice. Sacrifices to get rid of guilt: in Eskimo religion, in Hebrew religion (Day of Atonement). This leads to abstract sacrifice, the sacrifice of 'a broken and contrite heart': David after Nathan and the Bathsheba scandal: the sacrifice of time, talents, comfort, etc., for the sake of an ideal or profession – examples of this (e.g. Mum, doctors, pop stars and especially teachers!). The supreme personal sacrifice for the sake of belief: examples include Peter, Paul, Polycarp, Bonhoeffer.

6. *Religion as a programme of life*

What is a 'programme of life'? Exemplified by the alleged fascination of 'Coronation Street', 'The Archers', 'Mrs Dale's Diary', and other soap operas. The same interest has always been expressed in religion. Its connection with the major events of life.

Birth – beliefs and ceremonies in various religions: ancient Egypt, Yoruba and Ibo tribal customs, Navaho Indians, Hinduism, Judaism, Christianity.

Marriage – various practices; 'arranged' marriages and the reason for these. Jacob's marriage. Polygamy and its social and economic advantages and disadvantages. Polyandry treated the same way. Monogamy. Marriage practices in Judaism and Christianity.

Death – ancient ideas and practices; Viking burial ships, Egyptian ideas, Pyramids and their origin and purpose; the Hebrew idea of Sheol. The Christian idea of the conquest of death.

7. *Religion and the family*

Religion has always been closely connected with the way the family is run.

Family 'structures' among the pigmies, the Masai, the Ashanti, compared with 'the extended family' and the modern family. The reasons for each: groupings of fear and groupings of love.

The mother – in what ways is she important to the family? Her place in various religions. The father – similarly treated. Children – what are their rights and what are their responsibilities in the modern family? Their position in other religions, e.g. the place of the eldest son in early religion: Jacob and Esau.

This section has ancillary importance as establishing early the close link between religion and its subsidiary partner, morality.

8. *Religious 'language'*

How religion is transmitted. Various types of 'language'. A review of signs: pictorial, alphabetic, types of code. Ideas can be transmitted in all sorts of ways. This applies to religion.

By writing. What is the Bible? The Bible library. How we got the Bible: manuscripts, translation, printing, modern versions. The influence of the Bible – on art, music, literature, other religions.

By signs. Signs of fate in early religion: signs of the Zodiac, Aztec signs, Eskimo 'ducks' and 'ptarmigans', urim and thummim. The signs of various religions. The Christian secret sign: the fish – persecution under Nero and the signs used then and now.

By living tradition. What goes on in churches? What do the clergy spend their time doing? Where are the local churches? The history of Christianity in the local area – its arrival, spread and centres of influence. Local religious legends and traditions.

9. *The Strength of faith*

The end-product of the story of religion exemplified in several stories. Gideon, Mattathias, Barth.

10. *Conclusion*

The growth of religion – probably best presented as a summary diagram.

NOTE: Source-book useful for the teacher: B. Wigley and R. Pitcher, *From Fear to Faith*. It also contains exercises suitable for pupils, some further material, and is presented with an excellent visual impact.

'I see. Interesting. And quite demanding, too. He didn't tell you how to set about teaching it?'

'No. At least, he didn't himself. But then came yesterday's vision.'

'Ah, yes. Wednesday.'

'This time it was ... well, it seemed to be of some sort of a madman ...'

'Howdy, boyo! My name's Harry van Gogh. Wanna see a bitta howya do the ol one-two at the blackboard then? Bee-bop! Okay! Comin' up pronto: Speedy van Gogh, that's me!

Be – ddop – a – dopp – a – doo – dah – day'.

'See there? Instant Illustrations Incorporated. Day and night service. How to entertain your pupils in countless easy lessons. A bitta speed, a bit of imagination, a bitta humour, plentya coloured chalk, and Bob's your uncle! Great for the kiddies! New action-packed lessons and memorable diagrams can be yours ...'

'B ... b ... but ...?'

'Thrills all the year round. Give it 'em straight! Pow! Right between the ...'

'B ... b ... but.'

'Eh? Wassat you're trying to say, sport?'

'B ... b ... but ...'

'Yea, go ahead! Get a word in edgeways!'

'But what is it you're trying to tell me?'

'All I'm sayin', friend, is that if you wanna cheer up ya lessons

an' help ya pupils remember it all, one good way is by doin'
plentya coloured diagrams on the board.'

'But I cannot draw.'

'Nor can I neither. Fact I've seen eleven-year-olds do better than
me. But you can make up for that OK with humour and colour
and careful planning. Jus' don't be afraida makin' a foola yaself.
Go right ahead, an' you won't.'

'So you just put a diagram up on the board? During the lesson?'

'Sure! Why not? It'll only takea coupla minutes. You can do
it while you're talking.'

'I think I'd rather do it beforehand.'

'Ah, but the kiddies like to see it being done. Gets 'em interested;
so they remember it better, too.

Be – doop – a doop – doo, doopy – doo – doo.'

'... And they just copy it straight off the board?'

'Cripey, no! Wassa pointa jus' copyin'? That don't extend their
abilities, now, do it? Leave some parta ya diagram empty so as
they have to use their own imagination.

'Ya wanna see some quick examples? Okay then. But I'm
warnin' ya, these are complete ones. Now while I'm doin' these
I'll jus' tell ya that some are for the Form I syllable begya pardon
syllabus that ol' Wigley brought ya, and some of them are for that
Form II idea o' Bultmann's. They explain themselves okay. I
gotta scarper before ya first lotta pupils comes in. See ya!'

'Fortunately I didn't have a very busy morning, so I was able
later to take some quick sketches of the diagrams.'

'Thank you,' said Holmes. 'You would have no objection to
my keeping these for a short while for analysis?'

'I should be only too relieved to be rid of them. I'm afraid I
find their flippancy most distasteful and upsetting. They remove
every last shred of gravity that was remaining to my subject.'

'Indeed?'

'And now I believe we come to this morning's apparition?'

Before our very eyes, Holmes and I saw the tragedy of human
fear and degradation played out to its last syllable. The wretched
teacher, blanched and haggard as he was, began to shake and
gibber uncontrollably in his chair beside the chemicals.

BELIEF IN GHOSTS

ANCESTOR WORSHIP

RIP CHOW MEIN

BELIEF IN MAGIC

FETISHES AND LUCKY CHARMS

Primitive Religion was based on fear. (Form I)

Early ideas on why the world is here: an Egyptian view – the world
got here by accident when Ra sneezed. (Form I)

Ideas about gods: the Babylonians believed in a battle between the good god Marduk and the evil goddess Tiamat. (Form I)

Sacrifice as giving the best.   (Form I)

Stephen's preaching. (Form II)

Stephen's trial.   (Form II)

Stephen's death.   (Form II)

Manuscripts: Tischendorf discovers the Codex Sinaiticus.   (Form II)

The Buddha's mother's dream before his birth. (Form II)

'Get him a brandy, Watson.'

The alcohol appeared to fortify the unfortunate wretch; and in a few moments we were hearing of the last and perhaps the strangest of this terrible series of visions. It appeared that on that very morning, the vision had once again been of two men. One, it seemed, had been a Russian resplendent in furs and boasting a large black beard; the other, a dapper Frenchman with spotted neckerchief. Their names they had given as Boris Glasseyekov and Pierre Lavatour. They appeared to be engrossed in making repeated bows to each other, then ...

'Bonjour. Bienvenu to our présentation of les méthodes of RE.'

'Goodmorningski. Welcome to our presentation of RE Methodski.' More bows all round.

'In honour of the occasion I should like to recite an old Russian poem...'

'Psst!'

'On Nevsky Bridge ...'

'PSST!'

'Vot is it?'

'Not now, fool! You really do choose the most awkward times!' (To Windrush) 'You will excuse my friend. He is much upset by a recent visit to the oculist. So then, RE methods. What do you know about Elijah?'

'Well, he was a prophet, and he didn't get on well with King Ahab because ...'

'Is that vot you tell your pupils?' Boris begins to remove his hat.

'Yes ... because he had recently married Jezebel, who ...'

'Right now, God!' shouts Boris, frizzing his hair into disarray and threatening the deity with an extended forefinger. 'Now listen 'ere, God! What about this rain, then?'

'???'

'Well, you were talking about Elijah, weren't you?' explains Lavatour, flushed with delight. 'That's the way we think the topic should be taught.'

'???**!!'

'Tell him, Boris.'

'Classroom drama by the teacher – zat is the essence of our method. And you can apply it to almost any topic for lower school children, but especially to stories – and that includes Bible stories. Don't forget, after all, that they were often *told* as stories for many years before they were ever written down. So by their nature they are much better told – or, even better, acted – than read. A read story is a dead story. Come now, no need to look so bewildered. There are heaps of stories this can apply to. Think what a drama you could make out of the story of Oedipus, or of Christians in Nazi Germany, or of Nero and the fire of Rome, or of the life of the Buddha, or of Paul and the riot of the silversmiths, or of Joseph and the dreams, or of the call of Mohammed, or of the parable of the unjust judge; the opportunities of the method are endless.'

'You'd just look stupid.'

'Not in the least – not if you throw yourself into it. The people who look stupid are the people who do it half-heartedly or self-consciously. You only look stupid if you feel stupid; and you only feel stupid if you try to act without looking stupid. Do what you like (and if you're going to act all the parts yourself, you'll have to do quite a lot) – run up and down the room, speak in funny voices, pull peculiar expressions, close the curtains, stand on the desk, hide under your gown, scrabble on the floor; it really will work if you're prepared to make it work, and if these antics genuinely harmonize with the story. It really will work.'

'Hah! The mad Russians and the crazy French! You could never control a class if you did all that nonsense.'

'Naturally you have to establish your control first, but provided you've done that there should be no difficulties, and then your stories can leap to life. In fact this method is a great deal less risky than allowing pupils to do their own class drama – although we do sometimes allow this. But, the issue of discipline aside, this is a difficult technique to use profitably. Nothing but damage is done if the final standard of a class drama is no more than mediocre. So you must be prepared to give over several lessons to adequate preparation and rehearsal; and even then much will depend on the fluency of your pupils, and on keeping the level of embarrassment low. Considering all these difficulties, and the time required for class drama, we think that it is usually more practicable for the teacher to do the drama himself.'

'I'm fed up with all these idiotic syllabuses and methods. I'm going back to the Bible.'

'Well, look, mon ami; if you must go back to using the Bible, for goodness sake do it constructively. I mean, don't just carry on dishing out Bibles and reading round the class. Make your pupils do their own biblical research – on the stories of the birth of Jesus, for example. Get them to work out how much of the

Christmas-card image of Christmas is really justified by the gospels. Was there snow? Were there sleepy cows and asses? Were the oxen lowing? Did shepherds give Jesus their lambs? Is a stable mentioned? Did the shepherds see a star? How many wise men are mentioned? Is the same story in all the four gospels?'

'Pierre, look at the time!'

'Mon Dieu! We must go. No doubt you have a class waiting; we must not detain you. But we shall be back tomorrow to tell you more methods. Au revoir.'

'But just before ve go, I should like to take this opportunity to recite a famous Russian poem.

'On Nevsky Bridge a Russian stood ...'

'Come *on,* Boris!'

'Ach, Vladivostock!'

And with the wave of a wooden leg and the wink of a glass eye they were gone.

Windrush fell back in his chair, his fearful tale at last complete. Holmes remained silent and motionless, his head bent, his fingers pressed together, and his powerful brow furrowed with intense thought. The visitor shifted uneasily. Several minutes passed. At last...

'I have only one question to ask you, Mr Windrush. But I must caution you to take extreme care that you answer it as accurately as you can; the matter is of the utmost importance.'

'I shall certainly do my best, Mr Holmes.'

'Very well then. Now please consider: during the visions of the past week did you at any time – sneeze?'

'Good Lord, Holmes!' I ejaculated. 'This really is outrageous!'

'Kindly leave the matter to me, Watson.'

'But as a medical man I can assure you, Holmes, that there cannot possibly be the slightest connection between such harrowing spectacles and the degree of nasal congestion with which our client may be endowed. Indeed, even the most recent studies on the occurrence of influenza have shown ...'

'My dear Watson, I wouldn't dream of ignoring your professional opinion. Nevertheless I must repeat my question. Mr Windrush, did you at any time sneeze during the visions?'

'Come to think of it, yes! I believe I did. Every time, if I remember correctly.'

'Ah, that is all I wanted to know. Thank you, Mr Windrush. And now I think perhaps a visit to Crampton would be in order.

I take it you will be coming with us Watson?'

'Certainly not.'

'Not? Why, whatever is the matter?'

'I must tell you, Holmes, that nothing could be further from my intentions than that I should involve myself in the ghoulish machinations of these diabolical phantasms. And I consider that if you are wise you will discard all such intentions yourself.'

Holmes looked grim.

'No, Watson, I think I shall go. And as to the phantasms, I fear that, unless I am much mistaken, we are dealing with no mere demon or wraith, but with something much more sinister. If you are willing, I should be glad of your company. I advise you to come armed, by the way.' He turned to Windrush, 'Is the classroom much used on a Thursday?'

'I'm not sure. Not until two o'clock, I think.'

'Two o'clock! Then we have no time to lose! Quickly, Watson!'

An hour's train journey brought us to Crampton, an unattractive market town squatting sullenly in the East Anglian marshes. I must confess that I had been unable to shake off an unwelcome feeling of apprehension. Holmes however, appeared to be fully at ease; indeed, during the journey he had been positively jocular, to the considerable discomfiture of the wretched Windrush.

On arrival at Crampton Comprehensive we were shown to our client's classroom – Room D – where the fantasy of the past days had unfolded itself. Here Holmes became a different man, completely preoccupied with his examination of the room. He prowled carefully over the floor with his measuring tape, at times conducting minute inspections through his magnifying glass, the while uttering occasional grunts of satisfaction. I availed myself meanwhile of the opportunity to read some medical journals that had accumulated over the past year.

'Thank you, Mr Windrush. I think I have seen all I wish to see here. Dr Watson and I will now return to town for the night, and will see you here again tomorrow morning before the next vision. I assure you, there is nothing to fear. The mystery will, I think, be easily resolved. In the meantime, Mr Windrush, we bid you good day. I believe there is a train at three o'clock.'

We did not, however, take the train but returned instead to Crampton after traversing a number of fields by a particularly cold and muddy route. We booked ourselves in for the night at The Three Oaks Hotel.

I saw little of Holmes during the remainder of the afternoon and evening. From time to time he mysteriously came or went, dressed in green cap and blazer, short grey trousers, and invariably smoking his pipe. I guessed from his remarkable disguise that he must have been conducting some enquiries among the pupils of Crampton Comprehensive; but of the nature of these I remained totally unaware.

The next morning, however, we were up betimes; and after a good breakfast of bacon, egg, sausage, chips and beans, provided with diligent attentiveness by the lady of the house, we set off much fortified against the task confronting us. By nine o'clock sharp we were in Room D, and after a few murmured instructions from Holmes, Windrush departed for the school assembly while I took up my station crouching behind the desk at the front of the room. Holmes concealed himself at the back of the room beside the bookcase.

By 9.25 the RE teacher was back in his room, and sure enough, before our astonished eyes everything transpired exactly as we had heard it described. The room filled with coloured fumes; even Holmes and I began to sneeze and cough. Then before us stood the ghastly figures of Boris Glasseyekov and Pierre Lavatour.

'Goodmorningski. This morning we continue our talk on RE methodski.'

'Bonjour. Ce matin we continue our talk on les méthodes of RE.' Bows all round.

'And now for my poem: On Nevsky Bridge, a Russian stood, Chewing his beard for ...'

'Now look here, Pushkin! Pack it in with that poem or you'll be chewing your beard in the samovar.'

'Pfoo, Piskatchek! You never let me finish, you miserable one-legged, woodworm ridden Frenchman!' (Sulk.)

'Mon ami, you will please to excuse my companion. He is much disturbed by news of troubles in the Siberian glass-factories.

'Yesterday we talked about how to present RE to a class of lower school children. This morning we want to concentrate on how to set written work for the same range of pupils. How do you give notes?'

'Well, I er ...' stammered Windrush, 'I ... er ... I don't very much. That is, we don't do much written work at all.'

'Ai! Omsk and Tomsk! But how then do you expect your pupils to remember their work? Or to develop their written skills? Or to take your subject seriously?'

'I do sometimes get them to copy notes from the board ...'

'Ouf! Sacré bleu! But how then do you expect your pupils to learn to think for themselves?'

'... and I do set them essays ...'

'But how then will they get a sense of adventure? or of excitement? or enjoyment? Now listen to me. There are many many ways of making written work more enjoyable. You must at least have tried setting it in the form of letters, or newspapers, or conversations, or playlets, or radio-scripts, or TV scripts, or cartoon-strips? No? But these are almost as old as the hills. Well, they shouldn't be neglected, and they often work – provided you discuss some ideas first and don't just expect your pupils to do it without inspiration from you.'

'Certainement: and there are other methods that you can use, too. You can set work in the form of a press conference, or an obituary, or a book review, or propaganda leaflets, or posters. Have you tried using a tape-recorder? Very useful if you're discussing the nature of oral tradition. And what about recapitulation? Have you tried putting a series of lessons into the form of a household game? Here's one, for example on the life of Christ.'

'You should certainly have notes, of course. But they need not be boring or thoughtless. At the simplest level you can set a series of carefully chosen questions to be answered as fully as possible. But you should try to vary the pattern of work. What about writing sentences with blanks in? or setting anagrams? or getting pupils to put words and sentences into the right order? or putting the wrong second halves of sentences with right first halves, and setting them to sort out the mess? Use essays, too from time to time – but not invariably.'

'B ... b ... but ...'

At this point I regret to have to record the tragic spectacle enacted before us. For our client, who had by now been too grossly affected by his experiences of the past week, slumped insensibly to the floor. The Russian stepped forward.

'My friend, allow me to console you with a famous Russian poem: On Nevsky Bridge a Russian stood, Chewing his beard for lack of food ...'

'Non, non, non, Boris. You must not afflict him with this terrible poème. I suggest we play him some music.'

'Ach! very well, then. The usual, I suppose?'

'Mais oui! The Grieg piano concerto for solo recorder!'

Like lightning Holmes sprang from the bookcase.

A game which pupils can devise

useful method of recapitulation.

'Now Watson! Quick! Go for his leg!'

With due haste I propelled myself from behind the desk, but alas, only in time for a brief engagement with the rascals at the doorway. It was long enough, however, to determine that we were indeed dealing not with spirits from the netherworld, but with a peculiarly vicious and desperate pair of human imposters. The blackguards were too quick for us, and they clearly knew the school corridors infinitely better than Holmes or I. In a few moments we suffered the dismal experience of seeing them climb into a passing cab at the end of the drive, separated from us by a distance of at least a hundred yards.

'Holmes! Holmes! What a terrible misfortune! That such dastardly men should escape from our very hands! From our very hands, Holmes!'

Holmes chuckled.

'Good grief, Holmes! I can see no possible cause for amusement!' Holmes chuckled again.

'You must pardon me, my friend, for keeping you in the dark. I think that by now our two criminals will be safely in the hands of no less a man than Chief Inspector Baker.'

'But Holmes ...'

'You see, I realized that they might outsmart us and attempt an escape of this sort, and was fortunate in securing the services of my brother Mycroft as taxi driver ...'

That evening in Baker Street Holmes was relaxing in his chair over a glass of madeira and a pipe. We were discussing the strange affair of the visions.

'But how did you tumble to the plot so soon, Holmes? That's what I don't understand.'

'It was really quite elementary, Watson; quite elementary. I suspected the truth as soon as I knew that Windrush had sneezed.'

'I don't understand it, Holmes.'

'Think, Watson. What makes a teacher sneeze? Why, chalk-dust! The infernal fumes, then, were nothing but mere chalk-dust. So it was surely clear that we were dealing not with spirits, but with impostors. And it was a fair guess that they would turn out to be teachers themselves.'

'You mean, then, that the people Mr Windrush saw were not really Papias or Bultmann, or Jeremias or Dodd or Wigley or Van Gogh or Glasseyekov or Lavatour? That it was all a hoax?'

'Precisely so. I don't suppose that anyone of them bore much personal resemblance to the people they were claimed to be; though you must give them credit for attempting to make their point with an unusual dramatic device. But they finally gave themselves away by their choice of music. You see, Watson, Grieg never wrote a piano concerto for solo recorder!'

'Indeed? I'm afraid I'm not a musical man.'

'The only piano concerto he wrote was for – piano!'

'Why of course! Why on earth didn't I see it before? But one thing puzzles me, Holmes. What was the point of it all?'

'Yes, I too was puzzled by that for a while. But I found the answer when I discovered their identity. Perhaps you didn't notice the footprints in Room D? One was the print of a wooden leg. Or so it appeared, until I examined it closely. In fact it corresponded with not one known make of wooden leg. It wasn't genuine, Watson! It was a fortunate coincidence that I had myself recently completed my researches into wooden legs, which I intend to embody in a short monograph. I hope it will be of some small assistance to investigators such as myself. On discovering that the wooden leg was false, all we had to do was to lay our hands on a teacher who had no wooden leg. It was a reasonable guess also that his partner would turn out to be a teacher without a glass eye. I soon found that the only two teachers who answered this description were in fact, RE teachers.'

'So two other RE teachers were persecuting Mr Windrush?'

'You could put it that way. But I think they were themselves hoping to enlighten him.'

'But why did they pick on Windrush?'

'The pupils, Watson! Our client's pupils were so dispirited that they called them in to help. A little investigation among the pupils soon uncovered the scheme. You see, our client was really attempting to perpetuate the Sunday-school tradition of RE teaching into the secondary school. True, he was following the county's Agreed Syllabus for Religious Education, but it was very heavily biblical. You see, Watson, the agreed syllabuses were drawn up mostly by local clergy from all the major denominations, and the only thing they could all agree on was the Bible.'

'So, then, legally Mr Windrush was in the right?'

'Yes, indeed. But educationally in the wrong – as his pupils realized.'

'One thing has puzzled me all along, Holmes. How did you know that when he first arrived he had had to run to catch a train at Crampton?'

'It was really very simple, involving no more than a knowledge of the usual taxi fares here from all the London stations, together with a working knowledge of all train arrivals and an observation of the peculiar-coloured mud spattered up his trouser-legs.'

'It's truly amazing, Holmes! But tell me; how did you know that he was an RE teacher?'

Holmes chuckled. 'That was the simplest of all. He had been in such a hurry to catch his train at Crampton that he had quite forgotten to put down his Bible or take off his gown.'

4 What the Groundsman Saw

The watery sun begins to slip silently behind the cedars, and the autumn shadows grope their way across the playing field. Nearer the school, a thrush is cracking snails; a squirrel attends languidly to his nuts. Even the middle school[1] is held in the torpor of a Thursday afternoon. A groundsman pads by, his tools in his barrow. Inside also the senior master does his rounds, pressing a discreet nose to the glass partitions, and moving on. For each the classrooms pass by like a succession of so many lifeless showcases. History, maths, latin, geography, English. As the afternoon fades away, education congeals into taxidermy.

Little by little a discordant note edges its way into the consciousness of senior master and groundsman alike. A murmur; a chatter; a babble; shouting, banging, whistling, stamping; a howling, almighty riot. Where from? The room in the corner? Yes, look, it's bound to be; the blinds are drawn. It's the RE man playing with his audio-visual equipment again.

Like most riots it has grown from small beginnings and its roots lie in an unfortunate combination of poor judgment, incompetence, rebellion and panic. Things began to go wrong the moment the blinds were drawn.

'Now this is a slide of some Samaritans. What do you think they are doing?' A hand goes up in the front row.

'Yes, Graves; what are they doing? Oh, no, yes. Is it Graves? No, Brownson.' The penny drops immediately, if only in the subconscious of the class. He can't see what is going on. A girlish giggle comes from the mixed row at the back: 'You get your hands off me!' The teacher spins round and makes for the back of the room.

[1] In a secondary school 'the middle school' is a convenient shorthand term to denote the middle forms, i.e. the third, fourth and fifth forms which contain pupils of ages roughly 13 to 16.

'What's going on here?' A pointless question since the answer must be quite obvious. Some books clatter on to the floor at the front. A burly fellow in the second row now attracts the unfortunate teacher's attention by shifting suddenly in his chair.

'Was that you? Right, Deathridge, that's fifty lines you've earned yourself.'

'But oi aint done nuffink!' blares an indignant voice through the dark. At this cue, a chorus of indistinguishable murmurings begins to swell across the room, rapidly increasing in volume, and diminishing reluctantly only at the strident insistence of the teacher, now reinstalled beside the projector. With his first question unanswered and his first slide undiscussed, he goes hopefully on to the next.

'Now this is a picture of part of Jerusalem. Does anyone notice anything peculiar about it?'

'He's got a funny hat!' shouts a girl from beside the window. 'Hat! Hat! Haat!' The cry is taken up by a group of girls who promptly collapse in helpless giggles. The murmurings break out again. Somewhere in the room, someone starts whistling. Despite protestations by the teacher, the noise mounts. There is a clang as the waste-paper bin is kicked over by the door, and a scurry of movement indicates the onset of an impromptu football match. With a cry of rage and desperation, the now demented teacher launches himself towards the centre-forward, catching his toe on the projector stand. Amidst the crash of metal and glass, pandemonium breaks loose.

'Open the blinds! Open the blinds!' shrieks the voice from the floor. Suddenly everyone decides to obey; and, as the tape-recorder begins to trumpet forth Israeli folk-music, the lesson comes to an effective end with a stampede of the whole class across desks and chairs, in the intoxicating hope of being first at the blinds.

As the teacher lies in bed that night, mentally still thrashing face down in the tangled debris of educational equipment, will he at last see that slides and tapes alone are no solution to his problem? What gimmick will he turn to next? What new technique can he pull out of the hat? He pauses briefly to solace himself with the words of St Paul:

'The good that I would, I do not; but the evil that I would not, that I do ... O wretched man that I am! Who shall deliver me from the body of this death?' Inspired once more by the assurance that hope springs eternal, and feeling anew his vocation to suffer for righteousness' sake, he seizes on another possibility.

'Discussions! Yes – lots of discussions. Even Deathridge should enjoy that. It will have to be something they are really interested in. Let me see . . .' His mind ranges back over the sterile discussion periods of a few months ago.

'Do you agree that gambling is basically wrong?' Silence.

'Well, what do you think its dangers are?' Another awkward silence.

'Ya could lose yer money, couldn't yer?' says a girl.

'Yes. So do you think gambling is wrong?'

Silence. Then: 'S'pose it could be.'

This time it won't be gambling, he decides. Perhaps some other problem? Pollution? Shoplifting? Nuclear disarmament? Somehow they never went well either. Perhaps the children were not much interested in pacifism or the state of the environment. Well, then, something that will really fire their imagination this time.

'Sex! That's it, sex! . . . or perhaps drugs? . . . No, sex. They won't know so much about drugs, so I'd have to do a lot of the talking. Besides, there was that unsavoury business in the cloak-rooms last week. Yes, it's time we did some work on sex.'

And so the scene is set for another disaster. Not perhaps a riot on this occasion; but a disaster nonetheless when measured in educational terms. In a few weeks our teacher will have succeeded in convincing his pupils that both religion and RE are all about sex. And apart from this, what solid content will he have put over? Will he steer a middle course between embarrassment and flip-pancy? Will the discussion really lead to the moral regeneration of the school? And will he really be pleased to be known throughout the school as 'the RE-and-sex man'? Will the pupils have moved a little further in their use of written English? Will they really have developed a little more their capacity for logical thinking? An educational disaster looms ahead. Our teacher snuggles down in the bed-clothes, smiling peacefully as he slips into dreamland.

An unrealistic picture? Well, a little overdrawn, perhaps, but it is not basically inaccurate. RE teachers seem to go to absurd extremes when teaching in the 13 to 16 age range. If the extremes are not extremes of technique then they are extremes of syllabus. World religions and sociology become a panacea. One even hears of courses such as 'The life of Christ, studied on a sociological basis'. Quite meaningless. And almost everywhere there is an obses-sion with 'relevance'. Whatever is taught must be 'relevant'. But for some reason 'relevant' material has a way of turning out to be an irrational amalgam of current affairs and sex. The precise connection between the United Nations and abortion clinics, however, remains obscure.

Faced with such a crazy hodge-podge of malpractice and muddled thinking, we cannot avoid asking the question 'Why?' Why have RE teachers got themselves into such a mess? The answer is that they and a lot of other people have been taken in by a myth. A well-meaning aunt once wrote to one of the authors, 'I do not envy you your task, since the modern youngster seems not to have the slightest idea of even the Ten Commandments.' Here is the myth in its nakedness: modern teenagers are naturally hostile to religion.

It is of course an attractive idea in some ways. If you can't teach, blame the pupils or the changing times, or the pressures of modern life, or the decline of the family. We all know that the bad workman blames his tools; the bad teacher blames his pupils. But a myth contains a kernel of truth. You could say that it is a fanciful story made up to explain some fact that has been observed. So how has the myth grown up here? Where is the kernel of truth in this case? It lies in the fact that teachers have observed that teenagers are often hostile to RE lessons. From this they have spun the mythological conclusion that teenagers are hostile to religion. That teachers, the intellectuals of our society, should persistently fail to notice the howling *non-sequitur* of this argument simply leaves one gasping. Yet so it is; and the result is the current wilderness of trendy methods and non-religious RE.

To get at the real reasons for this hostility, a far more rigorous analysis is needed, and the first person to put under the microscope is the teacher himself. What sort of a person is he? A disillusioned vicar, trying to escape from parish life? A well-meaning amateur with no theological agility? A rejected ordinand? All very fine people, no doubt, but useless if they savour of disillusionment or piety, especially the latter. The slightest whiff of evangelism will put middle-school pupils off the subject. The one thing above all other that kills RE stone-dead is the teacher who tells his pupils what to think. He will immediately go down as one who is trying to 'put one over' on them. Quite rightly too, in our opinion. We oppose any method of teaching which stops children thinking for themselves. This, and not merely teaching concerned with religion, is what we understand by indoctrination. We think it is high time that the strictest demarcation were drawn between teaching and preaching. If you tell children what to think, you short-circuit the whole process of education. So who is to blame pupils who rebel? If teachers use RE lessons as an evangelistic platform or as a tool to make children behave, they have only themselves to take to task for the ensuing hostility. In fact pupils who reject this type of RE display a better understanding of education than their teachers.

The point can be taken a lot further than this. Middle-school hostility to RE is not just hostility to people who try to put one over on their pupils. It is hostility to the whole Sunday-school tradition of RE teaching: the odour of piety, get-out-your-Bibles, the lifeless waxy illustrations, the prayer shawls, the phylacteries, the pat answers, the sickliness and the boredom of it all. Once again, we have nothing but whole-hearted sympathy for pupils who reject this type of RE. If this is RE, we want none of it.

Then again, the system must come in for criticism. The supposedly 'statutory' requirement that one period per week of RE should be available to all children has been a deadweight about the neck for years, for it has led school hierarchies to assume that no more than this one period is needed. To the unconscientious teacher this means that lessons can be skimped (20 minutes instead of 35 if you can drag out the arrival and dismissal), only 15 lessons per class per term to prepare (and teaching the same topic to different classes over and over again). But to the conscientious teacher, the burden of marking, getting to know his children,[2] trying to use 35 minutes well (and what about the period 8 lessons?) is quite unbearable. If RE teachers have not always seen the stupidity of this, the pupils certainly have. In many schools it is taken for granted that RE is a waste of time. So it is, on one period per week.

Housemasters have not helped. It is very rare that they encourage their pupils to pursue RE at school to specialist levels or on into higher education. Even careers teachers frequently fail to see beyond the vicar image of theology at college or university. So we end up with a desperate shortage of trained theologians and RE teachers. Thus RE and its image deteriorate even further, despite the golden

---

[2] Compare the case loads of, say, a maths teacher and an RE teacher. Excluding all GCE teaching from consideration, we can assume that for 25 periods of each week, each teacher is dealing with classes of, say, 30 pupils. The maths teacher, probably seeing each class for 5 periods per week, meets 150 pupils in this time each week. But the RE teacher, who may see each class for only 1 period per week, meets 750. Yet both are expected to keep up to date with the marking of homework and both are expected to know their children properly.

opportunities waiting for those who want to use their theology in
original and constructive ways.

Nevertheless, it is time that some of the stink came to roost with
certain head teachers as well. How many have really taken the
trouble to try to attract first-rate RE teachers? And theologically
properly qualified RE teachers? You wouldn't expect a historian
to teach maths, so why expect a physicist to teach RE? Opportunities for secondment exist – why aren't the non-specialist RE
helpers sent on diploma courses in theology and RE? And how
many heads have really been prepared to give RE the scope it
needs on the timetable and in allowances for books? The headmaster who finds himself saddled with a crumbling RE department
may well have himself to blame. If he hears of riots in middle-
school RE, let him examine his conscience.

So teenage hostility to religion is really a myth. The kernel of
truth is that middle-school pupils are often hostile to RE. But the
reasons for this do not add up to hostility to religion; they concern
the nature of teaching and the position of RE in schools. The
trouble with a great deal of modern RE is that teachers have been
taken in by the myth, and have panicked. Thinking that they can
no longer teach religion, they have either given up 'teaching' – in
which case they have embraced ecstatically all the latest trendy
methods and educational knick-knacks – or they have given up
'religion', and so plunged head last into a jungle of ill-assorted and
exotic syllabuses. Others have just given up. All these people have
seen the symptoms of hostility, but they have made a false diag-
nosis. The result, of course, has been the wrong treatment.

'And now, good afternoon, ladies and gentlemen, welcome to
Hinchingbrooke. If you would like to take your seats over there
with the rest of the party, your guide will be along in just a minute.
Thank you very much. No, madam, there is no entrance fee; we are
not a museum. Your guide this afternoon will be one of our own
RE teachers. Here he is, and I hope you enjoy your tour.'

'Thank you, Rosa. Good afternoon, ladies and gentlemen, and
welcome to Hinchingbrooke. Will you come this way, please, and
I will introduce you to the school as we make our way to the
classroom block.

'We pride ourselves at Hinchingbrooke on our adaptability. The
very fabric of our buildings displays this inestimable virtue. You
will observe the harmonious blend of old and new. On your left,
ladies and gentlemen, you will see the house: originally a thirteenth-

century Benedictine nunnery, later the home of the Cromwell family and subsequently the home of the earls of Sandwich; at every stage adapted and enlarged. Now, in the latter half of the twentieth century, it has happily entered the era of Sixth-Form Centres, educational administration, and the stately homes industry.

'On your right you will not have failed to notice the streamlined, single-storey classroom block in tasteful shades of beige and white, the colour scheme here being subtly off-set by the picture windows and the grey plastic chairs. Ladies and gentlemen, I said we were adaptable. Here at Hinchingbrooke a stately home has become a comprehensive school. If that isn't adaptability I don't know what is.

'But this afternoon, ladies and gentlemen, you have not come to see the stately home. You have come to see the middle school and above all the RE room, with which my colleague and I are proud to be associated. So will you kindly step this way please? Up the steps and into the room directly facing you ...

'Now the first point I should like to draw your attention to, ladies and gentlemen, is the conveniently central location of the RE room. A pulsating centre of enthusiasm in the middle of the classroom block. Daniel in the lions' den, as you might say, ho ho. We at Hinchingbrooke like to think that RE is always a noticeable subject.

'Yes madam; RE is a very challenging subject to teach. But we are proud to boast that we have found very little hostility to the subject here. Yes; we like to think it is because of the way it is taught.

'Well, I'm afraid I can't agree with you there, madam. I know a lot of people think that teenagers aren't interested in religion. But our experience has been rather the opposite. Provided, of course, that you make sure that you are teaching it properly. Perhaps you will see what I mean as we take our guided tour round the classroom.

'In the north-west corner you will notice an interesting little collection of curios. Relics of a bygone age. We generally keep them locked up in case they should do any harm. Textbooks, ladies and gentlemen. A totally priceless collection, notable for its lack of interest. Each one a gem of evangelism. Yes, madam, by all means pick one up and examine it. Have you an eye for colour? I expect you'll be admiring the carefully selected shades of brown and muddy green with which these books were bound. Of course all the illustrations inside are black and white. Everything was very Spartan in those days, you know, right down to the quality of paper that was used. All done on the cheap, you see. Mind you, you have to remember that in those days boredom was the teacher's first weapon. Oh yes, everything was geared to that aim, including the books.

'No, sir; they are not entirely out of date. In fact, to let you into a secret, there is quite a market for modern reproductions of this style of book. For those that have a taste for antiques, of course.

'Why do we no longer use them? Well, sir, it goes back to what I said about each one being a gem of evangelism. Take a look at this series, for example. All about great Christians of the past. What was the point of these books? I can tell you what pupils thought the point was – an attempt at converting them. Not that they ever were converted. To them these "heroes" came over as cissy and sloppy, plaster saints, dull people with no depth or vitality. Besides, harping on the past never gives a good impression. The late head of religious education, ladies and gentlemen, unfortunately assassinated by a gang of professional comedians and now lying in Abraham's bosom, God rest his soul, always used to say, "Sonny," he used to say; "Sonny, the day you get to harping on the past, you're past harping at all."

'Talking of harping on the past, here's another series which does just the same: church history. But it's not what you or I would call proper history, not a balanced and impartial discussion of the past. This is just written to prove that Christianity pays. Well, sir, that's all right for bedtime reading; but it's not right for the classroom. I mean, it doesn't give a rounded education. And what about the omissions? The pupils soon spot what's been left out, and they don't stay interested for long after that. They think the book is slanted. And they're right.

'Over on this shelf you can see another series, one of the modern reproductions. The details are a little more up to date, but the basic pattern is the same. This series tries to present Christianity as a "challenge" – but look how wet the contents are.

'What it boils down to is this: we've had to lock these books away because they make RE look like church-going in school uniform. They're not objective enough.

'Now then, ladies and gentlemen, if you've finished examining the display of curios, perhaps you'd be so good as to follow me over to the notice-board. You will doubtless observe, in passing, the simulated coffee-stains on the floor tiles. We have taken great pains to reproduce for you in minutest detail the conditions in which an RE teacher might find his room at the start of a lesson. Assuming, that is, that some other subject had been going on first.

We find it's always a good idea to ensure our room is tidy. An untidy room produces an untidy lesson.

'Well, now, here we are at the notice-board, ladies and gentlemen. The history of school notice-boards is, of course, a fascinating one. Much time can be spent investigating the changing designs over the years. An ideal subject for an M.Ed thesis, I always think. The earliest extant notice-boards are of course late perpendicular; although there is some evidence to suggest that they were not unknown in the earlier Norman and Gothic styles. The Gothic Revival style is a popular one among some of our own better-known schools. Here, however, the architects have eschewed the more fanciful traceries and finials in favour of the functional design so prominent in later twentieth-century architecture. May I direct your attention once more to the colour scheme – chipboard in natural beige with white border – which harmonizes so well with the buildings as a whole.

'I expect you will have noticed the display exhibit no. 1 on the board: a typewritten copy of our recently introduced third-form syllabus. As this document may be of some interest, ladies and gentlemen, we have taken the trouble to prepare extra copies for you to take away. I'm coming round with them now. Thank you, sir. Excuse me, please. Yes, madam, this is the syllabus I was talking about. Of course, the pupils don't work from this, or hear all the big words either, but it's the basis of what's done in the classroom.'

RELIGION AND SOCIETY

1. *Religion and social order*

(*a*) The concept of social order. What laws does a society really need and why? Which laws are most important? The maintenance of social order: are the police pigs? Should they be armed? Is it reasonable to use guard dogs? Is torture ever justifiable?

(*b*) The close connection of religion with social order in many societies. 'Rites of passage' in African tribal systems. The importance of witch doctors as family psychiatrists. Taboo in Polynesia. Hindu caste system. Religious rulers: graves of Ur, evidence of belief that the king could lead his people through death; Dalai Lama and belief in his reincarnation, story of search for new Dalai Lama. Established religions throughout the world including Church of England.

(*c*) The connection of religion with the maintenance of social order,

especially in England. Prison conditions in the eighteenth and early
nineteenth centuries. The influence of religion in nineteenth-century
prison reform: John Howard, Elizabeth Fry. Consequent improvements: the silent system and the solitary system, prison trades
and treadmills. Were these really improvements? Twentieth-century
prisons – do they need further reforms? Punishment or re-
habilitation as their aim? Should capital punishment be restored?
Has the influence of religion on punishment been beneficial?

2. *Religion in mediaeval and modern society*
(*a*) Religion at the popular level – does religion equal legend?
And does it delude people? Mediaeval legends and beliefs: the
Grail, Parsifal, Glastonbury, Walsingham, Loreto, healings, relics
(Shroud of Turin). What was the appeal of these beliefs? Can we
accept them today? If not, why not? Are we free from legends
today? Pop stars, glamour created by the media; what are the
advantages and disadvantages of this? Publicity and public relations
consultants. Advertising and its techniques. Can the adverts be
believed? Propaganda. People make legends out of whatever catches
their interest. Religion at the popular level today: was God an
astronaut? Was Jesus a mushroom? A clinical examination of these
theories. Current interest in the Orient and the occult: Hare
Krishna, Black Magic, the Maharishi industry. What attracts people
to these? Modern popular religion: is it a form of opting out? Is
opting out a good or a bad thing? Hippyism. Conclusion: legends
and fashions are created by people, not religion.
(*b*) Religion and prejudice – are the two synonymous? Mediaeval
persecutions: the witch craze. Origins of witchcraft. Was Joan of
Arc a witch? Witch trials. Local evidence if possible, e.g. the
Warboys witches. Were the persecutions justified? The Spanish
Inquisition, and the persecution of the Jews. Reasons for antisemitism; was the Spanish Inquisition being 'cruel'? Contrast this
with modern attitude of Christianity: antisemitism in Nazi Germany, the Confessing Church. Particular attention to Bonhoeffer,
involved in secret service and privy to plots on Hitler's life. The
attitudes of Christianity to race relations: apartheid in South
Africa; right or wrong? Dutch Reformed Church in favour, Huddle-
ston and co. against. Same in USA. Origins of the negro problem.
Martin Luther King; compare the Black Power movement – who
had the better method? Religion opposing prejudice. But are there
modern examples of religious prejudice? Northern Ireland – a
religious problem or a political one? The persecution of the

Mormons; the suppression of scientology: were these justified? Conclusion: is there a difference between belief and prejudice?

3. *Religion and progress*

(*a*) Religion and education. Influence in origins of education. Monasteries and medieval universities. Indirect methods of religious teaching: symbolism, wall paintings, the origins of the theatre, examples of mystery, miracle and morality plays. Oberammergau. Modern religious drama: how successful is it? Nativity plays, etc., *Man born to be King*. The position of RE in schools today. The 1944 Act. The problem of assemblies.

(*b*) Religion and under-developed countries. Nate Saint and the Aucas – conversion to Christianity or the British culture? Can religion be naturalized? Morrison, Judson. Medical missionaries – Schweitzer. What is the role of Christians in under-developed countries?

(*c*) Religion and social reform. Slavery and William Wilberforce. Nineteenth-century factory conditions, child labour, and Lord Shaftesbury. Modern industry and its problems: trades unions – hero or villain? Is religion out of touch with industry? If so, why? Iona Community, worker priests. Are these a solution? Are they needed? Has religion any relevance to industry?

4. *Summary of the main themes*

Tea-time in the Nunnery Block. As this is a self-respecting guided tour, there has to be an opportunity for tea and scones. Sixth-form girls busy themselves at being hostesses, darting between the red-topped tables. Sightseers and guides have scattered themselves about the room, and now sit in haphazard groups. To the clink of white china and the gurgle of the urn, conversation breaks awkwardly out.

'Sugar?' A robust looking man in an open-necked shirt pushes the bowl in the direction of the guide.

'Not for me, thanks.' The sugar bowl is retrieved and the ritual of sugaring and stirring goes on in silence. The heavyweight takes the sacred first sip, and then issues his challenge.

'If you don't mind me saying so, I couldn't make head or tail of that syllabus of yours.'

The guide does his best not to ram a scone down the man's throat.

'Why is that?'

'I just couldn't see what it was getting at or where it was supposed to be leading. One minute you're talking about Glastonbury and the next you're on about pop stars and advertising. Quite frankly, it all seemed to me a bit of a muddle.'

Momentarily considering the possibility of following up the scone with an assortment of cups, knives, saucers and spoons, the guide contorts his face into a servile grin.

'Ah, I see what you mean. You don't like the way we have mixed different areas of the subject together: church history, world religions, moral issues?'

'No, I don't. It seems to me you're making the whole thing unnecessarily complicated. Why can't you teach in a normal straightforward way? Why can't you deal simply with religion, instead of messing about with legends and mushrooms and all the rest of it?'

'That's what we are doing, really. We are trying to get children to think about religion. The trouble is that they have a great many pre-conceived ideas. It's no good teaching them church history, for example, if their own basic attitudes haven't been discussed. So that is, in part, what this course is about. We try to get them to look at their own assumptions.'

'Such as?'

'Such as the idea that religion begins and ends with the church down the road. So we try to show them that religion is a worldwide phenomenon. That's why we try to bring in information about a wide range of different cultures: Nigerian, Polynesian, Mesopotamian, Indian. . . .'

'Well, if that's what your aim is I don't see why you can't teach them world religions in a perfectly straightforward manner, instead of mixing in so much else.'

'Have you ever tried spending a year, or even a term, on different world religions?'

'No, of course I haven't, I'm not a teacher.'

'In that case you won't have realized how desperately boring it is for the children.'

'I should have thought it was very interesting.'

'Yes, it can be for an adult who has an enquiring mind. But it is extremely difficult for children. The thought-world of, say, Buddhism is so vastly different from anything the pupils know, that they find it almost impossible to get into the swim of it. The imaginative leap is just too big. So it isn't really fair on the children to spend too much time on world religions as a separate topic. It just bores them.'

'Hmph; and what are all the rest of these preconceived ideas you say you're examining? So far you've only mentioned one.'

'One of the most important ones is the idea that religion is a backwater of society. A lot of children assume that it is absolutely insignificant, that it has no real impact on people other than church-goers. We try to get them to have a critical look at this idea.'

'And I suppose that's where the church history comes in?'

'Yes, in a way.'

'I thought you said earlier, when we were looking at those old textbooks, that you thought church history should be kept for bed-time reading. But now you're doing the thing you condemn – trying to prove how much influence the church has had.'

'No, I don't agree. And I certainly hope that we're not doing the same thing. I don't think we are, actually. For two reasons. In the first place, as I've just said, we are working with a much larger canvas. We're not just talking about the influence of the Church of England, or even of Christianity; we're talking about the influence of religion, all sorts of religion, all over the world. And in the second place, we try to be absolutely impartial. We don't set out to show that religion has had a good influence; we don't even try to prove it's had any influence at all. Our aim is to get the children to think for themselves and to decide what sort of influence, if any, religion has had. We think this is awfully important, you know. If you're not absolutely objective and impartial, you put the children off.'

'No doubt that's why you include things like the Spanish Inquisition, or the persecution of the Mormons.'

'Yes, exactly.'

'That's all very well, but you could still teach these topics in a prejudiced way, couldn't you? I mean, you could make the Mormons sound as if they deserved to be persecuted. Then you wouldn't be impartial any more.'

'I quite agree. That's the sort of topic which needs an absolutely dead-pan, clinical presentation, cold almost. The pupils will soon work out for themselves whether or not the Mormon ideas make sense. But one has to be fair. For example, there was a lot of trouble over Mormon polygamy; yet there was a case for supporting it, and the pupils need to be aware of this. It's no good telling them that Brigham Young had twenty-seven wives and then all laughing about it. That would stop them deciding for themselves whether the persecution was justified.'

'We seem to be getting away from the preconceived ideas. You say you are trying to examine the assumptions your pupils have. You've only told us about two: the point about broadening their view of religion, and this other point about discussing the influence of religion. What about all the rest of these preconceived ideas you say you are examining?'

'There are two others. They are both very common and very important. One is that religion is a pernicious influence because it makes people believe impossible legends. The other is that religious people as a whole are reactionary and prejudiced. We try to look at both of these.'

'They seem to me to be very abstract. Are you sure the children know what you're on about?'

'I suppose they are a bit abstract. But they're abstractions the children are very much aware of. Though of course they couldn't put them into words so easily.'

'I should have thought it was very risky to spend so much time on abstractions, myself. Don't you get bogged down in waffle?'

'Oh, no. After all, look at the syllabus. There's plenty of solid fact in it, plenty of things that the pupils know about and are able to discuss. We may be examining an abstract idea, but we try to do it in a pretty factual way.'

'I suppose it's in the discussions that all the moral issues get dragged in?'

'How do you mean?'

'Well, things like hippies, capital punishment, race relations and so on.'

'Yes; that is where subjects like these come in. But the "moral issues" are already "in" the rest of the material as well. These topics serve as a way of illustrating the issues a bit more, and bringing them closer to home. Besides, they bring a bit more variety into the syllabus, which is always very important for keeping the children interested.'

'But a lot of schools spend a whole term or a whole year on a really thorough examination of moral problems. I think that would be a lot more helpful, instead of treating them in this piecemeal way.'

'I know the system you're referring to. The trouble with it is that what you gain in thoroughness you lose in interest. After all, it really is rather dispiriting to spend a whole year discussing "problems". In the nature of the case, you can never come to any clear-cut conclusions – unless you bludgeon the class into agreement. Besides, if you follow this system you are implying to your pupils that morality is quite independent of religion. We think that is a false impression. Tramping back to the Bible for ready-made answers is no solution either; the Bible was never intended as an ethical supermarket. So we are always careful to integrate moral issues within a context of religious study. That gets the balance right.'

'Well, I'm not a religious man myself, but I think that the moral standards of religion are important; and I think it's a great pity that you don't concentrate more on that side of things. That would be something really useful to teach.'

'You mean you'd like us to use RE lessons to bludgeon our pupils into accepting a set of rules?'

'Oh no! I'm sure it could be done by discussion.'

'Provided the discussion came round to the right conclusion!'

'Well, you'd be able to wangle it somehow.'

'So it is bludgeoning after all, only this time the methods are to be more underhand. I'm sorry, but in our view that isn't proper education at all. And in any case, it won't work.'

'Your ideas on proper education seem to me to be a good deal too complicated for your own or your pupils' good. I still think you ought to be teaching simple things like morality or religion.'

'But morality and religion are not simple! And our ideas are not really all that complicated. If you boil them all down, what they amount to is this: in the past, people have taught church history, world religions, moral issues and so on as separate subjects. This made good sense from a theological point of view. Each is a separate area within religious studies. But it never made good sense educationally. These subjects, as such, never latched on to anything that the children were much concerned with. What we have tried to do is to use some of their subject matter, but in a format which really does deal with religious issues that are alive to the children. If they think religious people are always prejudiced, reactionary and stuffy, this is a religious issue that is live to them. So we have a look at it. And the same with the other assumptions we have talked about. You see, you can't expect to arouse their interest, or avoid their hostility, unless they can see the point of the course as a whole, however much the odd lesson may appeal to them.'

'Hmph.'

'And, of course, you have to be absolutely objective.'

Silence.

'Have another scone.'

'No, thank you.'

'Tea?'

'Hmph. Well, perhaps.'

Once more the silent ritual intervenes. Guide and heavyweight pause gratefully, to survey the room. The guide gazes absently at the next table. The extended finger of a tea-drinking lady begins to fill the cosmos. Then suddenly comes a croak at his side. His return-journey to reality drags him past a funereal walnut and confronts him with a wrinkled brown face. Surmounted by a black flower pot, it is balanced precariously on the apex of a heavy black overcoat.

'I beg your pardon?'

'I said, I've been listening to all you said.'

'Oh.'

'And I think you are putting yourself in a very dangerous position, young man. Very dangerous indeed.'

'How's that?'

'I don't think you're teaching RE at all. Well, you say you are taking great pains to teach impartially and you say that you do not want to evangelize among your pupils. But it seems to me that you are running the risk that your pupils may decide that Christianity is a bad thing – that is, if you encourage them to think so much for themselves. Surely, your job is to help them to see that Christianity is true?'

'The trouble is that you're just suggesting another sort of bludgeoning. To put it crudely, you want every lesson to come dragging up the church path.'

'But the young people can't really understand Christianity unless they know it from the inside. You must teach them to believe first, then you can teach them to think.'

'And what about other religions? Must they learn them from the inside too?'

'Oh no, young man. They're different. They're not as important.'

'Who says so?'

'I do.'

'Why?'

'Because Christianity is true. That's what I believe.'

'And what if I asked a Moslem for his opinion? Or what if the teacher were an atheist or a Jew?'

'He shouldn't be. This is a Christian country.'

'Is it? So it would be all right to teach Islam "from the inside" if we were in North Africa?'

'No ... Yes ... I don't know. That's different.'

'Well, are you arguing for Christian education as a matter of principle, or just because we live in England? I mean, if it's just because we live in England, then there's no religious principle involved at all. Unless you believe there is a special ethnic link between Britons and Christianity, and I don't suppose you imagine that. And if there's no religious principle at stake, I don't see how you can object to impartial religious teaching. On the other hand, if you are arguing on a religious principle then you're bound to suggest that Religious Education the world over should be dictated by the beliefs of one person – you. Are you prepared for that?'

Splutter!

'Furthermore, if education is, as we think, all about getting children to use their brains and to learn to think, wouldn't it be rather odd for the content of courses to be dictated not by reason but by faith? Besides, classroom evangelism doesn't work. It puts far more pupils off Christianity than impartial teaching does.'

The vanquished walnut subsides miserably into its bushes. The guide lifts himself to his feet.

'Now, ladies and gentlemen; if you have finished your tea I think we should be making our way back to the classroom block, to continue our tour of the RE room. Did you enjoy the tea?'

Reassured by the assenting chorus, he slowly leads the party back to the middle school and the tour continues. Notice board, blackboard, displays and filing cabinet one by one are gazed at and commented on. Further principles now emerge as the guide expatiates for, as he says, 'You can't live by the syllabus alone.' Any syllabus, no matter how interesting, which is not backed up by technical competence both in the classroom and in administration, is doomed to fall flat on its face.

The tour of the notice board is first of all completed with a brief look at exhibits 2, 3 and 4: timetables, lists of classes, and the exam timetable.

'Ladies and gentlemen; I expect you're thinking these exhibits are of no great significance. In one way you'd be right. You might find them in any classroom of any secondary school. But, ladies and gentlemen, closer inspection will reveal to you that here at Hinchingbrooke RE department they form an integral part of our Grand Plan.

'Now I can see you'll all be asking yourselves what we mean by a Grand Plan. Well, we're not planning to blow up the House of Commons. Just the House of Lords. Ho ho. No, but seriously; we

do have a grand plan for RE and divinity. Locally known as the
Divine Plan. Ho ho. Seriously, though, before I charge you extra for
all the jokes, I should like to introduce our local RE shop steward,
who is going to tell you all about the plan.'

A spiv-like character in checked flat cap and cheap car-coat
emerges and says ... 'Yea, well, fanks very much. Well, wot we're
arter, me an' me mates, wot we're arter is parity. Parity wiv ovver
edicational workers. Ya see, it's the status of RE we're concerned
abaht. We fink RE oughter get the same recognition wot ovver
acidemic subjicks gets. See, at the moment we're a special case, like.
Staff and pupils fink of us as somefink diff'rent. Vat's why yer
get some schools wiv a lotter middle school 'ostility to RE. But we
don't wanna be a special case, 'cos we want parity.

'Ave we taken any positive steps? We 'ave. Definitely. Over
the past few years we've been engaged in continuin' discussions
wiv management. An' I mussay they've been very reasonable and
agreed to most of our demands. Almost every pupil now 'as a
minimum RE workin' week of two periods; CSE and O level pupils
get three or four periods (over two years) and A level pupils get
eight periods per week. We fink this is a significant improvement.
Nobody could take any subjick seriously on only one period per
week.

'We've conducted a vigorous campaign to improve workin' conditions for pupils. Many schools 'ave a policy of makin' pupils
work in mixed-ability classes. We're proud to say that this doc-
trinaire approach to edication 'as been completely ruled out of RE
here. In every year except the first pupils are setted into classes
wiv ovver children of similar ability. Yer don't wanna mix up
pupils wiv an IQ of 130 wiv ovvers of only 60. Ya could never
satisfy and stimulate 'em all. Course, some edicational workers fink
yer can do it by subdividin' classes inter groups, or by givin' each
child an individle "discovery" project. But all this don't work
proper. I mean f're start, yer teacher a'n't got time to get rahnd 'em
all, so 'e can never know wevver they're workin' okay. And anyway, you've still gotter 'ave some class teachin' because if yer
teacher neglecks class-teachin' then you're deprivin' yer kids of
somefink important – the impack of an adult personality, see. Vat's
wot. We class-teach 'em in sets. Yer can't take RE seriously unless
yer get it at your own acidemic level.

'We've also 'ad constructive discussions wiv management on settin'
school exams. If you want RE to 'ave equal status wiv ovver
subjicks, then you've gotter set exams. If yer don't, you've not got

any standing wiv staff or wiv pupils. RE'll only be respected when it's allahed to be respectable.

'Wot's that? Yer don't fink settin' or exams is suitable in religion? Well vat's quite a common idea, but we don't agree. Yer don't wanna confuse religious belief wiv' religious edication. Intelligence don't matter in religious belief – and belief is somefink yer can't examine. Vat's true. But in religious edication – which is diff'rent – intelligence does matter, and yer can set exams.

''Ave we any 'opes fer the fewcher? Oh yes. Definitely. We intend to submit detailed proposals for the abolition of "general RE" in the middle school, and look forward to 'avin frank and constructive discussions wiv management on this an' allied areas of concern, an' ovver matters of common interest. Ya see, by the time the pupils reach fourth and fifth forms, they're gettin' ready for CSE and O level. So they lose interest in non-exam subjicks like "general RE"; yer can't blame 'em. So at this stage "general RE" becomes pretty-well useless, 'specially if it's only given one period per week. But this don't mean we want less RE. On the contrary, we want more. The best way to make it a successful subjick in the middle school is for all pupils to take it at CSE or O level, just as they do English or maffs, 'ist'ry an' g'ography. If all pupils are gonna do RE anyway (as we fink they should) let's make it worth their while. An' annuver fing. If A levels is to be de-specialized and sixth-formers is to take five subjicks insteada' free, we ekspeck more to do RE.

'Yes, of course the matter is still under negotiation, but we 'ope that an acceptable s'lution may be forfcomin' in the not-too-distant fewcher.

'So now to conclude, ladies 'n' gen'lemen. 'Ere we 'ave an RE department where we've made great efforts to gain acidemic parity wiv all ovver subjicks. The result is that there's very little 'ostility to RE. But now I'm afraid I must go as I 'ave an important works' c'mittee meetin' to attend ...'

Applause as the RE representative dons his cloth cap to leave the room. He pauses, as if their enthusiasm persuades him to stay and speak further, but looks at his watch, and hurries out. The guide resumes.

'Good. Now, ladies and gentlemen, we have just heard a bit about RE exams, so perhaps this would be a convenient moment to tell you more about them. Would you care to follow me to the filing-cabinet? This way, if you please. Thank you very much.

'You are now looking at one of our more recent installations, ladies and gentlemen. Introduced to the classroom block as recently as 1973, this triple-tiered filing cabinet has already made significant contribution to the teaching of RE. You will observe the elegant proportions and the overall simplicity of design which make this item such an attractive piece of classroom furniture. The cabinet is neatly finished in photographic grey and is equipped with an all-purpose security lock. Essential in view of the contents: examination papers.

'Now it's true that we do set exams for prestige purposes, but this is not the only reason; there are others.

'No, madam, strangely enough assessment is not one of them. In fact we consider this to be one of the least important reasons for having internal examinations. An exam cannot tell the observant teacher much that he didn't know already.

'The other main reason why we have internal exams is to keep the pupils keen. An exam can be a great morale booster, just as tests can. If pupils find they have done well, they are encouraged to work even harder. Of course this means that each paper has to be very carefully constructed. Each child should be presented with a paper on which he stands a reasonable chance.

'The result is, I'm afraid, that we set different papers for different abilities of pupil. Brighter children need a harder exam, slower children need an easier exam.

'Yes, indeed, sir. It does mean a lot of work preparing exams. But we think it's worth it if it keeps the pupils enthusiastic.

'Multiple-choice questions? Yes, sir, we do use them, but with great caution. Not like some people who see them as a way of giving the same paper to all abilities of child.

'I beg your pardon, madam? You don't know what a multiple-choice question is? It is the type of question where you have to select the correct answer from a number of possibilities. Let me give you an example from the filing cabinet . . . Yes, here we are: "The Greeks thought that the gods lived on Mount Olympus and their food was:

(a) Mars   (b) Ambrosia   (c) Locusts   (d) Aztec babies."
You would then have to tick whichever answer you thought was the correct one.

'But this type of question does have several limitations. For one thing, it is not entirely true that less able children find them easy. It's true that the questions do not demand such a high level of literacy, but they do require a very precise form of knowledge. For another thing, there are skills and areas of knowledge that they leave unused and untested. The children don't have to use their visual memory, for example, or display their literacy, or their ability to discuss intelligently, and select relevant material for their answers. Yet these are all very important skills which we should be trying to foster. And if we do not include these also in exams, then we are failing by that much to give our pupils an all-round education.

'Yes, that's quite right. We try to include a large variety of types of question in every paper that we set. Also it makes exam papers much more exciting and stimulating.

'How do we test visual memory? Very simply by giving the pupils pictures and asking them questions about them. And sometimes by asking them to draw a diagram or picture that they should have learned. The first of these is very useful in examining less able children. We have some examples here in the filing cabinet. Let me show you.

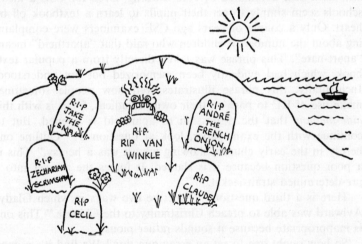

(a) Who was this man?   (b) What happened when he met Jesus?

(c) How was this man connected with pigs?

An exam question for children of lower ability.

'In a small way, this example illustrates a further point about exams. It's a helpful thing if you can introduce a bit of humour into your exam papers. The more the pupils enjoy your exams, the more they will enjoy your subjects.

'Essay questions? No, sir. They are not necessarily the easiest to set. Mind you, a great many people don't know how to set them. For example, I have here a copy of an exam paper I once saw. It was intended for third formers, and it consisted of nothing but essay questions. That's a mistake for a start, because it means that pupils can waffle for a whole exam. There really ought to be shorter questions as well, to tie them down to giving specific pieces of information. But look at the questions themselves! They're not excessively bad; but they are typical of the mediocre sort of exam papers which we always try to avoid. You should aim for excellence even in exam papers. Here, for example, No. 1: "Name two early Christian martyrs and say what you know about them." This is a very poor question. For one thing it is vague. For another, it tests nothing but the children's ability to reproduce their notes parrot-fashion. This is rote learning, requiring no independent thought by the pupils.

'Yes, sir. You would be astonished at how much RE in many schools is still dominated by rote learning. Even for CSE a lot of schools seem simply to get their pupils to learn a textbook off by heart. Only a couple of years ago CSE examiners were complaining about the number of children who said that "apartheid" meant "apart-hate". This phrase was taken directly from a popular textbook, which had evidently been memorized but not understood. Incidentally, this phrase illustrates well how people sometimes make use of RE to pass on their own prejudices, for it is with this *aide-memoir* that the discussion of apartheid is opened. But to continue with the exam paper, look at question 2: "Outline one heresy in the early church, showing why it was a heresy." This is a poor question because it is slanted. It forces the answer into a pre-determined strait-jacket.

'Here is a third question: "Describe two ways in which Gladys Aylward was able to preach Christianity to the Chinese." This one is inappropriate because it sounds rather pious.

'So how ought one to set an essay question? We find it's a good idea to give an essay question two halves, the first to test knowledge and the second to test the ability to think and discuss independently. For instance, here you can see some questions we have at times set.

1. What discoveries affected the mediaeval church? How did they help to pave the way for the Reformation?
2. What is Lord Longford trying to achieve? Do you support him? Say why or why not.
3. In what way would you reform church services? Why?

4. Write down all you know about Judas. Why do you think he acted as he did?

'This is just a quick selection, of course. We could show you many more from the cabinet, together with all sorts of other questions: completing a sentence with one word, or with several words; drawing; giving names, giving reasons, giving arguments in favour or against, giving brief descriptions of ideas or beliefs, giving six-line biographies – the list could be extended almost indefinitely. We always aim for great variety, and we try to challenge our pupils in as many ways as we can. If you can make your exams enjoyable, you can help to make your subject popular. Ingenuity and inventiveness always pay off.

'Now, ladies and gentlemen, I'm sure you won't want to spend all day admiring our exam papers and the filing cabinet, so perhaps you'd like to step this way to the blackboard.

'Here we have taken the trouble to leave intact for you two typical coloured diagrams that might be used during our work in the third form. Children always appreciate colour, ladies and gentlemen; it helps to bring the subject alive.

'Chalk and talk, madam? Yes, that's exactly what it is – a much maligned method of teaching.

'Yes, I know most people think it's boring, but chalk and talk as a method is neither more boring nor more interesting than any other method of teaching. What matters is the teacher himself.

'Look at the first of these diagrams. We have left them on the

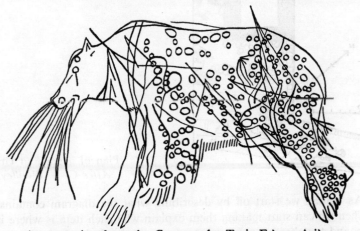

An engraving from the Caverne des Trois Frères, Ariège.
After H. Bégouen and H. Breuil.

board to show you what we think is one of the most important tasks
of the teacher, and one of the most important ways he has of getting
his pupils interested. He must make them think. His material
and presentation must be thought-provoking.

'We use this one to make our pupils work out for themselves one
of the aspects of primitive religion: hunting magic. After giving
a careful description we ask them to work out its significance with
no further clues. They have to deduce why early men drew this
particular picture and how it got damaged. Eventually, one can
arrive at a number of possible answers, one of which involves sympathetic magic. So we use this diagram, not as mere illustration,
but as a technique to make our pupils puzzle out the nature of early
religion. Here is another example of the same technique, this time
a plan from one of the "royal" graves at Ur.

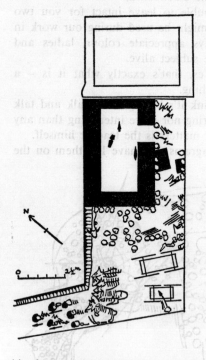

Plan of a grave at Ur.
After C. L. Woolley.

'As before, we start off by describing what the diagram contains.
Then we can start making them explain why each item is where it
is, and together we reconstruct, at a very simple level, the history
of the site.

'You think that this sounds more like archaeology than RE? Well, I see your point; but once we have worked out the story of the site, then the pupils can deduce something of what the people of Ur believed – about death, for example, and about the authority of their king. That's religious enough, surely? But the main point is that this technique gets the children thinking, at the same time as putting over good factual content. The subjects where children are made to think are the subjects they enjoy.

'Now will you please step this way, ladies and gentlemen, and we will show you the final item on our tour this afternoon, the display board. As every teacher knows, this is an essential item in the classroom. Children like to see their work displayed. It encourages them.

'Here, ladies and gentlemen, I should like especially to direct your attention to the variety of work we have been doing. You will observe the ingenious combination of diagrams, pictures, projects, essays, with newspapers and comic-strips. This of course, is just a sample of the many other methods used in the classroom. Naturally one cannot display a filmstrip, a discussion, or a tape-recording. We like to use as many methods as we can. Judiciously, of course.

'Yes, madam. I'm very glad someone noticed that. Yes, it is true that all the display at the moment concerns only one topic, religion and punishment. No, we don't think it is true that pupils get bored by concentrating on one topic. We find that as they grow older they need to study subjects in greater depth. In the first form we never spend more than two lessons, or perhaps three, on the same topic. By the time our pupils reach the third form, they often need two or three weeks on the same topic. Not more than that, however.

'We find that you have to strike a balance in the middle school between sufficient depth and sufficient brevity. If you spend too much time on a topic, you put your pupils off just as effectively as if you spend too little time.

'Yes, madam, it needs very careful judging.

'So the display board, ladies and gentlemen, shows once again how we try to keep our pupils interested; variety of methods, variety of material, and sufficient depth of study.

'At the beginning of the tour this afternoon, ladies and gentlemen, I tried to suggest that we at Hinchingbrooke are very adaptable. We like to think that this is so above all in the RE department. A stately home has become a comprehensive school, it is true.

But another transformation has taken place, too. RE, the boring nonentity of one period per week, has become an interesting and enjoyable subject. If that isn't adaptability, I don't know what is.'

The winter sun sinks slowly behind the cedars, and the autumn shadows lengthen across the playing fields. A thrush is cracking snails. A squirrel attends languidly to his nuts. Even the middle school is held in the torpor of a Thursday afternoon. A groundsman pads by, his tools in his barrow. Inside also the senior master does his rounds, pressing a discreet nose to the glass partitions and moving on. Silence. The afternoon drones on. But in the RE room, interest. Three o'clock and all's well.

> Cast a cold eye.
> On life, on Deathridge.
> Groundsman, pass by!

5 Breach of the Peace

The intercom buzzed and from it the disembodied voice said:
'Miss Davies for you, Mr Hardcastle.'

The personnel manager put his coffee cup down and, pressing the
reply switch, said: 'Send her in, will you.'

Within seconds his secretary, poised and confident, ushered into
the room a rather pretty girl, perhaps sixteen years old, the very
opposite of poise and confidence. An interview.

'Please sit down, Miss Davies,' said the personnel manager,
whose secretary unobtrusively glided out with the empty coffee cup.
Miss Davies smiled weakly, and sat down, hands clutching her
handbag strap.

'I see you've applied to join us straight from school,' continues
the manager with a reassuring public-relations smile, 'are you looking forward to leaving?'

'Yes, I err ...' she falters, trying to think which answer will
please.

'I see.' Pause. He looks at her application form. 'I see you've
four CSE passes,' he continues, 'but no maths.'

'No, I, well, I never could do maths. Only arithmetic, quick sums,
checking change, that sort of thing. All that algebra never interested
me.' She looks rather helpless. Why doesn't he ask what she can
do?

'Well,' he goes on, 'I see you have passed English, domestic
science, social studies and you've a grade 1 pass in RE.'

Answered prayer!

'Yes,' says Miss Davies, 'I took those last summer.'

'We haven't much use for vicars here,' laughs Mr Hardcastle.
'What was the point of doing a CSE in RE?'

'I was always good at RE and enjoyed it, so it seemed the
natural thing to do. Doing CSE gave me more chance to learn
about it.'

'Wasn't it just a case of learning off bits of the Bible?'

'No, we used to have interesting discussions about the Christian view of things.'

'That won't be much use to you if we employ you at this firm,' says the personnel manager. Poor Miss Davies is cornered. She has no qualifications in maths because she can't do algebra, clearly a barrier to employing her as a trainee salesgirl. She has been as good as told that the one subject she really did excel in is useless to her. And at sixteen years old, in a large executive office, among strangers and confronted by the well-meaning but terrifying interviewer, that's a lot to cope with.

'I always tried hard ...' she flounders. He isn't helping her at all. She fights the pent-up nerves that lead to tears. He sees a rather pretty girl, but uncommunicative and poorly qualified. A damsel in distress, who perhaps in the legends of bygone days would be rescued from the ogre by some gallant knight.

But writers can create and play God in their world of the pen. Rescue is at hand. The intercom buzzes:

'Two men, sir, to see you, a Mr Copley and a Mr Easton.'

'Tell them to wait, will you, you know I'm busy.'

'They say it's very urgent, in fact – come back' ... the voice tails off. The double doors of the manager's sanctum are thrown open and in rush two men. 'What on earth?' says the astonished interviewer.

'Answer the questions and you won't get hurt,' says one of the intruders, Donald Easton, in impeccable Oxford accent.

'Now,' says the other, Terence Copley, and with more than a hint of Yorkshire accent, he goes on, 'we ask the questions and you answer them.' They look menacing. Miss Davies cowers, forgotten, in the background, as the two invaders grab the astonished manager by the lapels.

'Why are you picking on RE?' says Copley.

'Because as an exam pass it's useless,' is the spirited reply. The two hoodlums exchange glances.

'Tell me one subject that is useful,' says Easton.

'Maths for a start.'

'What use is the geometry, algebra, computer work and all that except to mathematicians?'

'Well, it trains the mind.'

'And what use is French?'

'That's useful if you ever go to France for a holiday.'

'Five years to get what a phrase book can teach you in two weeks?'

'Well, you get other benefits,' says the interviewer, now interviewed.

'Such as?'

'It trains the mind.'

'Does history?'

'Yes, I suppose.'

'Then why can't the same be said for RE?'

'Because RE's different.'

'Why?'

Stubborn silence.

'Surely RE is just as useful (or useless) as all these subjects. It may lack direct practical application, but it makes the child think, helps him to come to a view of religion of his own; after all we all have religious views or anti-religious views all our lives. Perhaps this is, in a way, the only school subject relevant to life after school – how we live from day to day depends on our values and attitudes. . . .'

But a promising lecture is cut short. Neither will history ever record the manager's answer. The tables are now turned on our authors. They are about to be captive, for while they've been tackling the interviewer about his attitude to RE as an exam qualification, the secretary has telephoned the police. A burly man in blue enters the room. This is Chief Inspector Baker.

'I have reason to believe that you are causing a breach of the peace,' he says; 'I shall have to ask you to accompany me to the station for questioning!' They are led out, leaving Mr Hardcastle to straighten his tie.

'Silence in court.'

'Terence Copley, Donald Easton, you are charged that on the fifteenth day of July 1973, you did wilfully enter the premises of Mammoth Merchandise Ltd. and did cause there a breach of the peace, using intimidating behaviour against James Helperby Hardcastle. How do you plead?'

'Not guilty.'

'Not guilty.'

The prosecuting counsel, Sir Denvers Drage, rises to address the court. 'The facts of this case are very simple, m'lud. The two defendants burst into a private interview and used intimidating behaviour to one of the parties. They were apprehended there by Chief Inspector Baker and taken to the police station and charged. They signed there a statement in which they openly admitted that

they entered the office and behaved in a way which could be con-
strued as intimidating, but claim that they were quite justified by
the circumstances. I think we can agree on the actual events on the
day in question without the need to call further evidence.' The
defendants nod their assent.

'No doubt they will argue in court,' continues Sir Denvers, 'that
the circumstances of the case justified their actions. The defence
will argue that Mr Hardcastle was discriminating unfairly against
Miss Davies in assuming that her CSE RE qualifications did not fit
her for employment. They will therefore have to convince the court
of the value of such a qualification. The crown will demonstrate
its worthlessness ...'

Sir Denvers drones on. Mr Justice Windbagge shifts uneasily on
the bench. Flatulence – and more. Why do these RE men persist
in taking the thing seriously? Why, if this happens in RE up and
down the country, children might enjoy it ... A level sets might
treble and quadruple in size ... Where would it all end? No, an
example must be made of these men at once ... Trying to get RE
accepted like any other subject ... and then having the nerve to
conduct their own defence.

The voice of counsel pierces his reverie, '... so, m'lud, the
crown calls as the first witness the filing clerk from the CSE Board
offices.' A rather harassed looking man is sworn in. Prosecuting
counsel turns to him and says: 'Will you explain to the court
the procedure for examining CSE candidates?'

'Yes,' says the mouse, 'there are three types or modes and the
school chooses which they will enter. In Mode 1 the syllabus is
externally devised and examined; in Mode 2 a group of schools
submit a syllabus and scheme for assessment – the CSE Board has
to approve it and then moderate the results; in Mode 3 an individual school submits a syllabus for a course and assesses it, with
external help. Less often a group tries 3 or an individual 2.'

'Which procedure is normally followed in RE?'

'Mode 1.'

'So most RE candidates normally sit Mode 1 papers?'

'I have no nationwide survey to hand, but I should say that
this is so, yes.'

'Will you give the court some examples of CSE Mode 1 questions
you have seen?' The little man takes out a dossier from a battered
briefcase and supplies the following, which are listed as exhibits: [1]

[1] These have, in fact, all been set (but by different boards) in recent
years.

1. Which of the following best represents the Christian teaching?
(a) Punishment should fit the crime
(b) Think of the criminal, not the crime
(c) All crime is a sin against God
(d) The criminal is a victim of circumstances
2. Do Christians object to Sunday sport? (one sentence answer)
3. What is the Christian judgment on euthanasia?
4. 'Peace at any price.' What do you think of this slogan? What is the Christian answer to it?
5. Make a list of talents God has given people. How can a Christian use these in God's service?
6. Why was God displeased with Eli?
7. Write out the commandment that says that we should respect our parents.
8. Write a letter to Cliff Richard indicating your approval of a pop-singer who sets a good example to modern youth.
9. 'For I do not what I want but I do the thing I hate.' Give an account of a day in your school week which shows this remark to be true.
10. How important is prayer in our lives? In what way does it affect our lives?
Does it make any difference to the way we live? Give your views.
11. How should friends behave towards each other?
12. Why does the church worship God?
13. Where does evil come from? (15 minutes for this essay)
14. Describe how pagan superstition was overcome when Christianity was introduced to Britain.

'There,' says counsel, vindicated, 'now will you read the rubric on this paper to the court?'

'Candidates will be given credit for expressing their own personal views.'

'Wogs go home? I submit that these questions are indoctrinating, over-simplifying and misleading. CSE passes based on this sort of thing are worthless.'

Stirring in court, murmurings in the public gallery.

'Do you wish to ask any questions?' says the judge to the defendants. Negative response. The two defendants sit mute and still. Damaging evidence goes quite uncontested. More murmurings.

'The crown therefore submits that Mr Hardcastle's assessment of Miss Davies' suitability as a potential employee was perfectly reasonable and that there are no grounds whatsoever for justifying the conduct of the defendants. The crown rests, m'lud.'

Mr T. Copley opens the defence case, without a speech, and calls his colleague as the first witness.

Q: What do you see as the main weaknesses of CSE RE on Mode 1 syllabuses?

A: The biblical papers seem trapped in the straitjacket of the 1930s Cambridgeshire syllabus, which of course takes no account of recent strides in other branches of RE, or even the guide-lines suggested by Ninian Smart for the Lancaster Project.

These aims are entered as defence exhibit no. 1.

The work will be guided by the following principles:

1. Insight should be given into the role of religion, and in particular the Christian religion, in the formation of British Society.
2. Insight should be given into the nature, challenge and practical consequences of religious belief.
3. Account should be taken of the pluralism and actual practices of people both in contemporary British society and in the wider world.
4. Religious education should be open, rather than dogmatic; and should require honesty of conviction, of whatever kind, in the teacher, without infringing the right to developed freedom of choice in the pupil.
5. Religious education should be both relevant to the experience of the young and designed to broaden their experience towards an understanding of the religious dimension in human culture.

Q: Let's turn now to the list of CSE questions produced in evidence by the crown. What do you think of questions such as no. 3, on the Christian view of euthanasia, or Sunday sport?

A: I think it's extremely difficult to coat the pill of modern life with Christian sugar, by treating the Bible like Old Moore's Almanac and digging out bits that are supposed to show the Christian view of euthanasia or abortion or whatever.

Q: Do you see any future in this sort of question and approach?

A: None at all, if RE is to survive as a fitting study for people of all sorts of persuasions and backgrounds.

Q: Can you see any alternative to it?

A: Yes, I can. I don't think we've used Mode 3 half as effectively as we might have done. Here was a chance for syllabuses to be tailor-made to the needs of a particular school. Much more enlightened syllabuses can then be used.

Q: But will CSE Boards approve them?

A: They have done, and are doing.

Q: Why is Mode 1 surviving at all, then, if Mode 3 has so much more potential?

A: Well, a Mode 3 syllabus takes enormous preparation time, and serving teachers are always pushed for time. Then of course, there are treacherous headmasters –

The court perks up.

Q: Treacherous headmasters?

A: Yes, they like to switch children from CSE to O level classes or vice versa – or even teach CSE and O level in the same class – which means an identical syllabus for both.

Q: Why is that so bad?

A: It makes the CSE a diluted O level, quite contrary to the spirit of the whole thing, and then you have an inflexible syllabus.

Q: Can you give the court an example of the sort of Mode 3 syllabus you would use?

A: Yes. This is the Copley-Easton syllabus. Of course it's far from perfect, but it performs a number of useful tasks, giving insight into religion as well as Christianity, and showing something of the religious picture in Britain, and as you can see it involves the class in a lot of the contemporary debate.

This syllabus is entered as exhibit no. 2 for the defence.

Paper 1 (compulsory): Religion in the Modern World

Section A
The distribution of the main world religions, Hinduism, Buddhism, Judaism, Christianity, Islam. Their numerical strengths with problems of measuring these. How do we define a Christian? Any baptized person? An occasional church-goer? The different ways in which members of these religions worship and their use of scriptures.[2] Any study of doctrine would only be such as was relevant to this. Use could be made of the new material for schools on world religions. Then religious language, myths, parables, symbols.[2] Finally the question, Is man a religious animal? Everyday superstitions, turning to God in crises, caring for others.

Section B
Religion in Britain. Has organized religion declined during the period 1870–1970? Possible discussion points: the Darwin clash, effects of two world wars, problems of material prosperity, appar-

ent decline of authority. A study of the church's response to this, the ecumenical movement, changes in worship, the church's contribution to social and pastoral work, industrial missions.[2] Finally a look at problems raised by new sects,[2] Jehovah's Witnesses, Mormons, Spiritualists, Christian Scientists.

The overall aim of this paper would be to present living religion as something much bigger than the Bible, or the church down the road, but in which both Bible and church play their part. This could lead either to Paper 2a, Biblical Studies, or 2b, Religion in a Particular Area. In different ways both these papers follow on from the material covered in Paper 1.[3]

Paper 2a: Biblical Studies
The origin and growth of the Bible. Modern translations.[2] The different types of books in the Bible: history, law. A study of several types (not to gain detailed text knowledge but to appreciate the type of book, writer's aims). Texts would be allowed in the exam. Perhaps a gospel (Mark), a letter (I Cor.) and a prophet (? Amos). Finally why Christians value the Bible, how the canon evolved to protect the church, the Bible's influence in different ages and religions.

Paper 2b: Religion in a Particular Area
Ideally this would be the student's own area. Obviously we can't give here more than the general lines such a localized syllabus should follow. A heavily industrialized area with much of its past obliterated would have to consider recent history and the present position in much more detail. Areas with a high immigrant population could extend their researches beyond Christianity. There is much scope for the individual student to follow aspects that interest him, even in schools not offering formal projects, in which local religion can be a rich field. But all students should examine the present, as well as the past, and this paper is not intended to be the dissection of a fossil! Clergy could be interviewed on their view of the role and future of the church, services could be analysed etc., the activities of a particular church could be studied in detail.

CSE Boards that were too harassed to construct a detailed syllabus along these lines would have to ask their local college to do it for them, no doubt an exercise that students and tutors would welcome!

[2] Material suitable for project work.
[3] Material requiring class discussion runs throughout the whole paper.

In conclusion, we must remember that the CSE (and probably O level) student would benefit from work in a much wider area of religious studies than is now the case. It is only after a broader introduction as suggested earlier that depth studies such as synoptic gospels can be profitably attempted.

The mark weighting would be 60-40 (Papers 1 and 2) or 50-30-20 (Papers 1, 2 and project)

Q: I should like to draw your attention to the prosecution list of questions, no. 6, 'Why was God displeased with Eli?' Do you consider that this sort of question could be asked on your syllabus? 'Why was God displeased with Amos' contemporaries?', for example?

A: It could appear, but only if the person setting the exam paper was very unsubtle. You see, it begs the question of who or what or even whether God is. A much happier way of phrasing it would be 'Why did Amos believe that God was displeased with his contemporaries?' That doesn't beg the God-question.

Q: Do you find other value judgments in these questions?

A: Too many. These ought not to dominate questions at all, if you'll excuse my making a type of value judgment. For example, in the prosecution sample, questions 7 on respecting parents, 5 on talents and even 14 implying the worthlessness of pre-Christian religion in Britain all imply very definite value judgment. This is also obvious in their question 8 about Cliff Richard.

All these could be eradicated by a careful re-wording of the question, though too often, I'm afraid, it's been simply a re-echo of what the classes have been taught.

Q. Do you see any other major dangers in these questions?

A: Yes. I was horrified by question 2 on Sunday sport in one sentence, or the one on the origin of evil in 15 minutes. I'd like to know myself what the answer to question 1 is. It's all over-simplified to the point of absurdity.

Q: Couldn't your syllabus be examined in a similarly disastrous way?

A: To be perfectly honest it could, but it should not be. Teachers who use Mode 3 have two major priorities, first to get a suitable syllabus, and second to have the exam framed in such a way that value judgments and over-simplifications are minimized, that the opinions of pupils should not be examined – how can you assess and grade two people's opinions? Anyway, we don't want moral tribunals.

Q: So what do you advise?

A: Blood, toil, sweat and tears – there's no short cut, though local colleges could help out a bit with syllabus construction; it *would* probably be a welcome exercise for staff and students.

Q: Could Mode 2 help this problem by getting groups of schools together?

A: Well, when different schools get together it's useful to compare notes and techniques and produce a joint syllabus, as in Mode 2, but in practice the meetings are sometimes hard to arrange and the syllabus isn't quite as tailormade for your children as Mode 3.

Q: But you prefer it to Mode 1?

A: Almost anything is preferable to the way in which Mode 1 has been used.

Q: Thank you. I have no further questions

The prosecution can now conduct their cross-examination of the witness:

Q: Our witness, giving an expert opinion on which mode of CSE most schools enter, said that he found that in RE most entered Mode 1. Would you dispute this?

A: Like him, I haven't done a survey, but I think his opinion is probably correct.

Q: Does this not show that they prefer Mode 1 to Mode 3?

A: That's a matter of opinion. As I said, they may not have time to prepare a new syllabus, submit it to the board and so on.

Q: Come now, you don't expect the court to believe that. The schools prefer it. Teachers are conscientious on the whole, and if they wanted Mode 3 they'd use it more.

A: I don't agree there. Teachers spend a lot of time on marking and preparation, but it doesn't leave them a lot of time to plan syllabuses and long term objectives. It's easier to concentrate on day to day survival.

Q: But as you say, your view is no more than an opinion. Let's look at your Mode 3 paper. I believe you said that your syllabus involves classes in contemporary debate about religion?

A: That is right.

Q: Would you agree that the status of morals is an important feature in contemporary religious debate?

A: Yes, that's true.

Q: Well, would you tell the court why so little on morality appears in your syllabus? It doesn't live up to its claim to be adequate, does it?

A: We see moral education and RE as inter-connected. We think the recent rush to moral education has been by people reacting against your sort of Mode 1, only they've over-reacted.

Q: And that also is only your opinion isn't it?

A: No, because secular moral education with no religious content represents a tiny element in modern theology and doesn't correspond to society as it now is, with religious and moral attitudes still very much intertwined.

Q: Don't you think you should include more ME to prepare people for 1984?

A: I'm not a person employed to change society. My job is to help children to look at religious and moral attitudes and form their own views about the sort of society they want. ME is a healthy correction to the sterile sort of RE you've been talking about, but you mustn't kill the patient with an over-dose of drugs.

Q: I still don't see much ME on your syllabus.

A: I concede that. But very often ME comes out of what is being taught – in other subjects as well as RE – and the sensitive teacher tries to use these spontaneous chances to explore some sort of moral or ethical dilemma. It's much less forced than, say, going into a class and announcing that 'We're all going to talk about pre-marital sex'. And you can't overdo ME on an exam syllabus without problems of assessment. Are you going to have a question such as:

Abortion is (a) right, (b) wrong, (c) sometimes right, (d) a matter for a private decision?

How can you set about marking it?

Q: Hmmm. Let's go back to employers. Are you seriously suggesting that they should welcome CSE RE?

A: Yes, as part of a good general certificate showing competence in different but significant areas of human activity such as language, the arts, science and religion.

Q: Don't be naive, Mr Easton. Look at the bald facts. Do you think employers will change?

A: Some have, and more will if we can get them to see what the point of RE is.

Q. How do you propose to do that?

A: (modestly): I'm no miracle worker, but I hope at least that accounts of this trial will show them something. And I hope some teachers will try our Mode 3 syllabus and see for themselves how it works.

Q: You sound confident?

A: It seems strange to me that CSE RE has too often been left behind, in view of some of the break-throughs made in other branches of the subject. There's a terrific opportunity to work with groups of young people who really are interested in religion – and most young people are, even though they wouldn't describe themselves as religious. Their work should be acknowledged in some comparable form to their work in other subjects. This is our stake in CSE.

Q: And you're the man with the answer?

A: I should be rash to claim that; but I am claiming an insight.

Q: (dubious): Hmmm. No more questions.

The defence makes a brief summary statement:

'The prosecution has attempted to prove the worthlessness of qualifications in CSE RE. We submit that the evidence brought by the Crown, although representative of certain styles of CSE RE, is certainly not representative of the best. We therefore submit that it is contrary to natural justice to deny employment to an applicant on the grounds that CSE RE is a poor qualification, and claim that our entry into Mr Hardcastle's office was entirely justified by the circumstances. The defence rests, m'lud.'

'Members of the jury' – judge summing up – 'this is a curious case. The prosecution have produced evidence which clearly points to a bad exam record in CSE RE. The defendants do not deny this. They submit that this bad record need not be perpetuated, and they have produced in evidence a syllabus which (they claim) supports their view. You must decide how far their syllabus answers their own questions about the Mode 1 system. The prosecution case strongly implied that in a society like ours a qualification in moral education would be more appropriate than one in religious education. This hint was important, members of the jury, because if the Crown is right in this, the whole *raison d'etre* of the defence view of RE collapses, since the employer would be in the right. On the other hand, the defendants may be right to claim that moral education cannot stand on its own feet, for they seem to be saying, if I may put it like this, that R does not equal M. Is M alone, as they contend, an absurdly or unnecessarily secular view? Or would it be possible to construct a five-year course of ME with clearly defined aims, which was examinable in an objective way; and if so, could it really claim to supersede the defendants' view of RE? Might it not also partake of the "dilution" to which the defendants have referred, so common in all CSE subjects in an attempt to make concepts clear to the less bright child, but which can be dangerous and harmful in RE? The crown has contended that RE has been presented in such a way that it cannot claim the serious attention of employers as an exam pass. You, therefore, have to judge whether the sort of RE proposed by the defendants will provide children with a qualification sufficiently valuable that a prospective employer who disregarded it could be considered guilty of an injustice. You are not here to judge RE on its past criminal record, members of the jury; you must weigh the defendants' case on its own merits, not on the memories of RE as you have received it. Ladies and gentlemen of the jury, the verdict is yours.'

6 Wot's on Telly?

A crowded staff-room. Coffee cups, cigarette-smoke, books. Sounds
of prosperous laughter. Snatches of conversation:
  'So I said to the head ...'
  'I'll make a decision when the estimates come through ...'
  'But his essay-style is remarkably good ...'
The camera tracks in on one particular group. While the group
talks and laughs a youngish teacher, ill at ease, hovers around
the edge looking for a gap. From time to time he smiles ingratiat-
ingly at one of the others, but is ignored. He carries a Bible. The
group talks:
  'I say, George, how are your A level pupils coming on?'
  'Oh, I think they should be okay. It's always a struggle at this
time of year, of course, but ...'
Voices fade out as young teacher turns away, disappointed.
Colleague comes up and puts a hand on his shoulder.
  'You know, it's time you got some GCE pupils yourself. You
haven't even got an O level set, have you?'
Young RE teacher looks soulful and chews lower lip.
  'If you had O and A level classes you'd be a new man. Think
of the prestige your department would have! Why not give it a
try, eh? If I were you, I'd go and ask the head right away!'
Burst of laughter attracts colleague back to group. RE teacher
hesitates a moment, then with new look of confidence and enlightenment turns and marches into group himself.

  'And now here is a party political broadcast on behalf of the
Parliamentary Divinity Party.'
Camera shows front view of speaker, hands clasped confidingly on
desk. The desk is neat apart from some casually placed Dinky
toys. A man-to-man smile.
  'Hello. Over the past few years the number of youngsters staying
at school to take exams – O levels and A levels – has gone up

enormously. Now this, of course, is exactly what we said we were
going to do when we came into office, and we've done it. And
that's not all. Because we're now having serious discussions which
may lead to radical changes in the exam system of this country.
One possibility is that we may get rid of A levels altogether. Now
I can see you'll all be asking, "Why get rid of A levels?", and
that's a very good question. But you know, this country – and
we've made it absolutely clear that this is a country – has been
producing thousands of school leavers every year who know far
too much about their subjects. So what we're thinking of doing
is to introduce an altogether new type of exam system to enable
all these youngsters to learn less about more instead of more about
less. But this is all in the future. What we're really concerned about
at the moment, and this is something which concerns everyone
of us – the man on the shop floor, the industrialist, the property-
speculator, nurses, teachers, miners, old age pensioners (suppressed
sob) and the lower paid – what we're really concerned about is to
see that RE keeps the firmest possible foothold in the exam system
of this country, whatever shape it takes.

'Now people sometimes ask me, "Why should we have O and
A level exams for Religious Education anyway?" and this is a
jolly good question. But you know what we really need to see is
far more people taking exams in RE, not less. And what this
country has got to do is to make jolly sure that we all pull together
and that we don't stop pulling till we've got there. You see, let's
get down to brass tacks, right at the grass roots level. We all think
about religion, don't we? Even if we don't believe it. So it's really
a question of whether we think clearly or not. We don't want our
children to grow up like the sour-faced men who think they have
all the answers. You've got to know what the problems are before
you can discuss religion properly. And that's what these exam
courses are all about – teaching people how to think about religion.
And you know, they're not just for the pious or for people who
want to be vicars. They're for anyone and everyone; and I can
tell you, we've got some jolly good courses. And when these young
people really settle down and get on with the job they find that
there are all sorts of things they never knew about: manuscript
problems, questions of historicity and historical perspective, questions of morality, questions of philosophy, and much more; and it
all helps them discuss religion in a more informed, more incisive
way.

'So you see, what we want you to do is to help us keep this policy going. It's a good policy, it's a fair policy, it's a moderate policy; and above all it's a successful policy. But at the end of the day, when all's said and done, it depends on your support. I hope we can count on you. Goodnight.'

'That was a party political broadcast on behalf of the Parliamentary Divinity Party.'

'Join your local O and A level RE courses for *Herod*! *Herod*: the full-blooded, swashbuckling, epic story of the most daring and most powerful man in Jewish history!

'A story of intrigue ...'

Camera cuts to sumptuous oriental interior: silk drapes, cushions, arabesque windows, golden stools. Herod relaxed and smiling, threatens prisoner who stands bound and gagged. 'You see, Minutius, we have ways of making you talk ...'

'... of violence ...'

Night scene in alleyways of Jerusalem. A figure walks hurriedly up deserted alley, keeping to shadows. He turns a corner. Thud. Sound of scuffle; blows, grunts, moans. Then four men return round corner and flee into the night.

'... of excitement ...'

Brilliantly lit semi-desert. Yells and shouts off-stage. Then on to screen charge thousands of oriental warriors. Flashing scimitars, flaring nostrils, stumbling horses, clouds of dust as the stampede passes camera. Picture holds like this for at least a full minute. Screams continue.

'... of oriental splendour ...'

Cut to magnificent building with terrace, colonnade and flight of steps leading down to open square. Square is filled with excited, jostling crowd. Soldiers hold crowd back. Trumpet fanfare. Herod and elaborate retinue step out of building on to terrace. Crowd goes mad with sustained cheering. Enthusiasm. Herod waves regally. Close-up of Herod as he speaks out of corner of mouth to nearby sycophant: 'Tell Ben Zakkai he must do nothing till I give him the signal ...'

'... the tragic story of the decay of a noble mind ...'

Night-time in the palace. Herod's bedchamber. Tapestry curtains, heavy candelabra, the flickering of candles. Alarm bells ringing in distance within palace. Camera shows Herod in nightshirt, haggard and slavering, grey with fury, pacing the room. He shouts at attendant, 'Do I have to find him myself? Do you care nothing that your king is plagued nightly with murderous assassins?'

'But Majesty ...'

'Find him this instant I say!'

'But majesty, we have already looked and there is no intruder.'

'Don't lie to me, you impudent, lily-livered, pock-marked scum! Are you too turning traitor against me? All right then; where have you hidden him? Eh? Eh? I'm warning you, find that intruder or I'll have your milk-sodden gizzards ripped from that eunuch's belly and pulped for pig-swill! Where is he? Where's the assassin?'

Picture fades as Herod lunges dementedly round the room, looking under bed, behind curtains, throwing over vases, pulling down tapestries, etc.,

'... and the story of a woman ...'

Cut to small chamber, candle-lit, elegant. Remains of meal à deux: bowls of fruit, wine jug, golden goblets. Two couches. On one reclines voluptuous woman in flimsy, revealing gown and gold trinkets. Sitting close on same couch is Herod.

'Oh Herod!'

'Mariame!'

They embrace passionately. Heady music intervenes.

Herod! On show regularly in your local O and A level RE lessons. Don't miss this golden opportunity! Enter today for exams in RE!'

Studio picture of announcer.

'And now, *Weekend Story*; and today's story is taken from a new book of short stories by Heather Rose, and it's called "Not for me the heavens". Here to read it is Olga Whitford.'

Fade in the tinkling of a musical box. Scene opens on a Florentine patio; a small fountain gurgles in foreground. Camera enters spacious conservatory decked with obviously sweet-scented climbing flowers, and containing various pieces of white-painted, wrought-iron garden furniture. Olga Whitford is poised on a seat. She smiles and opens a book.

'Now there was a certain RE teacher, and he was clothed in long black gown and fine linen jacket, faring sumptuously everyday on soggy cabbage and suet pudding, and putting his feet up in the staff-room: and a certain beggarly examiner named Macallister was parked at the school gate, full of bitterness and cigarette ash, and desiring to be given the exam scripts from the RE teacher's O and A level candidates; yea, even the traffic wardens came and stuck tickets on his windscreen, and the dogs watered his bumpers.

'And it came to pass that the examiner died, and that he was carried away by the syndicate into the chief examiner's committee room: and the RE teacher also died, and was buried. And in the Infernal Classroom he lifted up his eyes, being in torments, and seeth the committee room afar off and Macallister in a deep, black and chrome, leather-upholstered, swivel chair. And he cried and said, O Chief Examiner, have mercy on me, and send Macallister, that he may dip the tip of my pen in red ink and help me mark these books; for there is no end to the mistakes therein and I have no ink. But the chief examiner said, Not so; for thou in thy lifetime didst take thine ease and not one of thine exam candidates has done well; yea, they have all failed, even unto the last of them.

'But how can this be? answereth the teacher, seeing that I have dictated to my pupils many notes in the two years, yea also for revision? And this year we have even finished the syllabus.

'And the chief examiner reproacheth him and saith, I know thee how thou teachest. Wherefore dost thou only dictate notes? Knowest thou not that the whiles thou dictatest thy pupils may think on football or girl-friends or the pop scene? And hast thou not heard that discussion sharpens the mind and awakens interest? But wherefore are thine O and A lessons so dull? Seest thou not the value of humour and drama? Thinkest thou only to lecture? Truly thou shouldst not so have taught, for that way lieth the serpent of boredom and the chasm of low morale.

'But thou, when thou givest notes, seek not after a transcription of thine own words; but do thou first talk and then give to thy pupils an outline with clear headings. And so shall they build whereon thou hast provided the framework. And for an ensample of good notes, behold is it not written in Appendix III?

'Think not that thou canst prepare thine O and A level lessons from day to day. For to such as take no heed unto the morrow to them also shall the morrow take no heed; for his pupil staggereth into the exam room confused and bewildered; yea, he knoweth not the question that cometh, neither hath he completed the syllabus.

'But thou, when thou preparest thy lessons, plan first the whole syllabus and then shall each lesson fall into his place. And be not bound by the syllabus, for unto O level pupils shall be given an increase of interest and understanding by him that prepareth an introductory course, such as that which I shew unto thee.

O LEVEL INTRODUCTORY COURSE   FORM **IV**
(approx. 1 term)
HOW TO STUDY RELIGION

General Aims: to show
  (1) how religion should be studied
  (2) how 'big' the subject is

1. *What is religion?*
Influence of religion in history and now on art, music, buildings, books and people. Statistics of major world religions.

2. *What is history?*
The need to examine the bias and reliability of sources. Desirability of reaching original sources where possible. Illustrated from mediaeval Arthurian legends, contrasted with the real Arthur. Similar tendency to eulogize 'saints', e.g. Neot, Ivo. The Bible's 'bad press' for one of Israel's greatest kings, Omri; cf Assyrian account. Why did he receive only one paragraph when his fame was remembered by surrounding nations for centuries? Popular belief that Jesus went about claiming to be God or Son of God; contrast this with the synoptic view that he used deliberately vague term 'Son of Man'. Popular belief that Jesus was meek and mild; contrast this with actual gospel information – overturning money-changers' tables, controversial character, etc., Jewish bias of Matthew's gospel contrasted with Gentile bias of Luke – structure of the gospels.

3. *Archaeology and the light thrown on religion*
Egypt – pyramids: the gods and death. Beliefs about Ra and Isis. Assyria – human-headed winged bull, Gilgamesh, sacred plants and shemesh. Early Christian religion in England – Lullingstone Roman villa mosaic. Engraved christening spoons, crosses, destruction of pagan wells. Jewish religion – lack of images in excavation confirming their commandment. (Filmstrips available.) Masada. Bible cities.

4. *Texts*

Who were the scribes? How were texts stored? (Dead Sea Scrolls.) Rylands fragment of Fourth Gospel. How do we date them? The need for linguists – Greek New Testament, Hebrew Old Testament, Sanskrit, the Koran. Aramaic background to NT. Comparison of different manuscripts. New discoveries leading to new translations. AV replaced by NEB.

5. *Language*

Scholars help in translation but also in explaining terms like Messiah, Christ, Buddha, from comparison with other records.

6. *Views reflected in art*

Stained glass: used to educate, but shows how men through the centuries have 'read into' Jesus. How do we interpret Christ in our culture? Other examples: statues of the Buddha, Chinese depiction of Christ, Sutherland tapestry, initiation masks in African religion, Blake's Ancient of Days, French cave paintings, Chartres cathedral.

7. *Philosophy and religion*

Man always asks the question 'Why?', 'What is God like?' The 'proofs' for the existence of God. Socrates encouraging people to think for themselves and to ask. Was he right?

8. *Living people and tradition*

Passing down information and ideas. Communion-rail in churches deriving from mediaeval anti-canine protection in the days when churches were open to all. The surviving Samaritans. Jewish Rabbi and his teaching method. Nursery rhymes preserving belief. 'Mary, Mary', 'Jack and Jill' (Norwegian religion), 'Ring a ring o' roses' explained. Women wearing hats in church. Bad things passed down: Mohammed and the Jews, leading to Israeli-Arab hostility.

Why is Jewish Sabbath the seventh day, not the first?

9. *Primitive people now*

These sometimes provide evidence of early religious belief. New Guinea, Voodo, Pigmy. Their use of music, belief in sympathetic magic, sacrifice. Comparison with some Old Testament passages.

10. *Emotion*

Love, fear, hate – can be examined objectively but not explained away. Is religion like this? An awareness rather than a mere opinion or intellectual belief? Religion as a matter of decision, not opinion.

11. *Summary*
The complexity of the material. Religion is alive!

'Neither teach the biblical texts from their first chapter even unto the end, for so the commentaries love to do. But thou, when thou teachest them, reorganize them according to their chronology, their themes and their secondary material, and so shalt thou diminish their editorial confusion. But take heed lest in so doing thou confuse thine own pupils; therefore to each shalt thou give a printed sheet which sheweth thy scheme of work. And when thou teachest non-biblical subjects consider the past papers, how they are set. For from them thou mayest learn much and plan thy scheme of work.

'And the rest of the works of the O and A level teacher, behold are they not written in Appendix 3?

'And the teacher said, I pray thee, therefore, O Chief Examiner, that thou wouldest send Macallister to my school where I taught for I have five colleagues, that he may testify unto them, lest they also come into this place of torment.

'But the chief examiner saith, they have the appendices; let them read those. And he said, Nay, O Chief Examiner; but if one go to them from the syndicate they will improve their exam teaching. And he said unto him, If they read not the appendices neither will they be persuaded though one went to them from the syndicate.'

Fade in musical box again as Olga Whitford closes the book, looks up, and smiles. Fade out.
Studio picture of announcer.

'That was Olga Whitford reading "Not for me the heavens" by Heather Rose. And now for something completely different.'

Scene opens on busy school locker-room. Senior pupils coming and going with books and files. Noise of locker doors banging, pupils talking and whistling. Slick man in suit stands near doorway, holding microphone. He faces camera.

'Pupils everywhere are changing to exams in RE. We tried to find out the reasons ...'

'Excuse me, madam' – he accosts a girl – 'I see you're carrying some books.'

'Yes, that's right. I'm just off to a lesson.'

'Have you got any RE books there?'

'No.'

'Don't you specialize in RE?'

'No. I'm studying ... (bleep) and (bleep).'

'Have you ever thought of taking an exam in RE?'

'An exam in RE? Tee hee! Don't be silly!'

'You mean you've really never thought of it?'

'Well, no, I suppose I haven't.'

'Why's that?'

'I don't know. I've always done (bleep) and (bleep).'

'Why not have a go at it now?'

'Well...'

'Have a try!'

'Well ... all right ... I'll give it a try.'

Girl disappears into classroom. Picture of commentator.

'We gave Aileen Carter one lesson of RE and one ordinary lesson to see if she could tell the difference. And here's what she found ...

'You've tried both lessons?'

'Yes I have.'

'Which did you think was better?'

'Oh, the second one. It was so much more lively and exciting and the revision plan was so good.'

'Tell us about this revision plan.'

'Well in the first subject the teacher just said we could start to get on with our own revision and he would leave us alone in all lessons and homeworks for the next two months until the exam.'

'And in the second lesson?'

'In the second lesson the teacher discussed it all with us and we decided to have a short test every lesson and to plan it out so that we cover the whole syllabus in our two months of revision. He also wants to see our revision notes to check that we're keeping up to date with the work.'

'And you liked the second idea better than the first? That sounds odd!'

'Not really, I think the first plan sounds very boring. I think we'd all get depressed before the exams start. And there's no way of checking how you're getting on, or of making sure that you keep up to date. But the second scheme will make certain of all that, so we really will know everything. We're all very pleased.'

'And you're not going to be given revision notes by the teacher?'

'No. He says that more notes would confuse us.'[1]

'So if you had to choose, which of these two subjects would you take?'

'Oh, the second without a doubt!'

'And you have chosen —— RE!!'

(Gasp of astonishment and delight from girl.)

'Now; you have chosen RE, but are you sure you've made the right choice? Just to test you, we have here one GCE exam paper in RE, and exam papers for two other leading, cut-price subjects. We're going to offer you the chance of doing *two* exams for the price of the *one* RE exam. Will you accept the offer?'

'No, I'd rather keep the RE exam.'

'We'll offer you the two exams *and* a chance to poison the head of history!'

'... (hesitates) ... No. I'll keep the RE exam.'

'And Aileen Carter is confident that with RE she'll be able to pass her exam. That's why pupils everywhere are changing to RE.'

Cut to studio. Picture of announcer again.

'And now before we close down for the night, here is Bill Raven with the outlook for pupils' prospects in the next year or two.'

Camera shows grey-faced, grey suited man with floral tie, standing in front of unintelligible charts and maps. He attempts a leer at the camera.

'Good evening. Well it'll be generally bright throughout the period though there may be duller spells here and there. We're expecting a slight depression to settle over pupils in June and July due to the prevailing exams, but this is quite normal; and in fact with the good planning and revision we've been having temperatures should be rather lower than usual for this time of year.

'Now we've been having occasional seminar papers and lecturettes over the past year, and reading has been increasing steadily with guidance in some parts. Over essay-style there have been occasional storms but coherence is moving in now and we're getting attention to detail as well.

'So looking further ahead, to September-October, when there's generally a marked movement of pupils into colleges and universities, the outlook remains bright. This time of year usually brings some rather gloomy periods and this is due to the higher pressure we generally get. But with the reign of guided independ-

[1] For a more detailed discussion of revision techniques see **Appendix III.**

ence that we've already had, and with the steady build-up of self-
help, we're hoping that this autumn we shall be able to avoid the
usual floods of tears and missed opportunities.

'So the general outlook is for no more than mild depressions in
June-July, and a bright outlook for the following months into
the following year.

'And on that cheerful note we end our forecast and indeed this
evening's broadcasting. This is Bill Raven wishing you a very
good night. Goodnight.'

                              National Anthem.

7 And For Our Next Trick

Six people at a table. A Tussaud-like stillness. Only the smoke from one man's cigar shows that they are not indeed wax. The atmosphere is heavy with smoke and resignation. A committee meeting. Hours of Minutes. Reams of Agenda.

'He that endureth to the end shall be saved.'

An explosive cough from the cigar smoker is intended to remind the others that his time is valuable. After all, he is Colonel A, whose crisp military tones order the greengrocer, newspaper boy, taxi driver or whatever unfortunate crosses his path 'at the double'. As churchwarden he is used to committees. As ex-army he is used to command. But he is a genuine person and a respected, if not popular, man.

Next to him sits Lady B. Back from opening some gala or fete she is come to this meeting and sits, sabled, glowing and ready for business. B Hall is known for its charity and none within its walls more liked than Lady B.

On her left is the local vet, Dr C, a quiet, shy man, who says little, but gives the impression of thinking a great deal more than he talks. Opposite him is Councillor Mrs D, who says all that she thinks, and more. Next to her is a vacant chair, hence the late start of the meeting.

At the head sits the chairman, and to his right another man, a headmaster, or rather 'the' headmaster, for this is the governors' meeting.

'The first item, ladies and gentlemen, is this rather unusual request from the RE department for an extra £250 a year allowance to start now in the current year.'

Quizzical looks.

'The head of RE has sent a detailed note to try to justify this on the grounds of the need for new textbooks and group work material in the light of the obsolescence of existing stock. Can you throw any light on this, headmaster?'

'Well,' says the head, 'I know he was wanting me to write off 400 or more Revised Version Bibles as dead stock. No local church wanted them. He said he'd asked the caretaker to burn them but the caretaker told him he wasn't a religious man but he drew the line at burning Bibles.'

'What the devil's the fellow up to?' says Colonel A, 'Does he want to burn the £250 as well, to show God defeating Mammon?'

'His answer,' says the head, 'is that he doesn't use the Bible in class, apart from exam work' – Colonel A reddens – 'because he says it's not written in children's language and it confuses them.'

'He what?' expostulates the Colonel, 'I suppose his ideas are better than the Word of God. I'll tell you why we've got so much hooliganism about these days, and long-haired yobboes, it's because damned RE teachers are failing to give them a Christian upbringing, that's why it is. Instead they get this chit-chat hogwash. Teach 'em the Bible. Tell this chap to do his job properly.'

'That sort of RE didn't do us any good,' says Lady B, laughing. 'You've no moral right to indoctrinate children in a maintained school, and anyway, it doesn't work. Look how our generation rejected it.'

The veins in Colonel A's throat bulge ominously.

'Now, Vera,' he says, 'look here, the truth is the truth is the truth. This chap Copland, or whatever he's called, has got to put it over to the kids. That's what it's all about.' But her ladyship is not to be bullied.

'No, I think you're over-simplifying, Henry. I think the real problem is "What is the truth?" This man's task is to introduce the children to the debate in an informed way, so they can make up their own minds.'

'They're not mature enough,' retorts the Colonel, chewing hard on his cigar. 'I suppose you'll be joining the Votes at Eleven Brigade next.'

'They will make up their minds, whether you like it or not,' Lady B grins.

'I think you're both missing the point,' says Mrs D, who had endured non-participation for long enough. 'Religion is dying out. You've only to look at the churches to see that. Yet we're being asked to subsidize it in school. This is pointless. We'd just be trying to preserve a fossil. You've got to move with the times. We've been asked to subsidize a subject that's on the way out. RE should be quietly merged with history and social studies.'

The head thought longingly of a neighbouring school where the staffing difficulties in RE had been solved by abolishing the subject and then proclaiming it as part of the humanities course ... after all, the course included a bit of church architecture! Lady B returns him to the debate.

'That's all very well, Mrs D,' she says, 'but you're actually assuming the same thing as the Colonel, that the RE teacher is a vicar-figure.'

'Well, how do you see him?'

'I think he's trying to impart information about religion, not inculcate belief; correcting all the misapprehensions and strange ideas children have picked up and involving them in the current debates about human responsibility, life after death, and so on.' The Colonel blows his nose expressively.

'Let the Social Studies or English department do that,' says Councillor Mrs D.

'I doubt if they've the expertise on the religious side, and anyway, I should imagine they're asking different questions about events and interpretation.'

Dr C interpolates: 'Personally, I think the reason why people ask "Why RE?" is that they've been badly and boringly taught. Here's a man who's trying to interest the children instead of passing on his own religious conviction, or lack of it. I say, give him the money.'

Mrs D dives in again. 'Then they'll all want more.' The power of cash ... stronger than philosophy.

Lady B intercedes. 'Think of the mess we'd be in without adequate RE resources or staff. Children would be left with the garbled accounts of newspapers, doorstep vendors of religion, even churches.'

'Rubbish,' from the Colonel, a churchwarden.

'Oh, Henry,' she says, 'what a picture children get at services. A man in a milking smock looking deadly serious ascends the pulpit, six feet above contradiction, as John Robinson says. The adults round about in various postures of indolence and decay, till he's finished. And Sunday schools have different aims, poor resources, and don't reach the majority of our children anyway.'

Colonel A changes tack. 'Well, it's the parents who should bring up the child to know what is right ...'

'Yes,' agrees Councillor Mrs D, 'and RE can be phased out.'

'But parents don't do that,' says Lady B. 'They haven't the capability to deal with all the religious and moral questions – their silence often means that their children only inherit apathy towards religion . . .'

'Which goes to show,' says Dr C, 'that your RE man here is right. He is saying that you find religion the world over. Look at it. Learn about it. Think about it and decide eventually if you want any part of it. Personally, I'm a humanist but I strongly support this sort of approach.'

The chairman looks at the late arrival for a moment, but he has not so far spoken and is forgotten by the others. He seems quite engrossed in the spectacle he is observing.

'Perhaps,' continues the headmaster, 'I could tell you what he wants the money for . . .'

'No,' interrupts the chairman, 'that's his business. The principle is what matters. Do we lend him more than generous support? What is our priority to be? You see on Item 4 the Out-door Pursuits Club are asking us to subsidize a holiday on Anglesey.'

Dr C can't sit through this. 'So you rate two weeks for 40 children more important than giving help all the year round towards more effective teaching of 1000 children?'

'We aren't a holy club,' says Mrs D, 'so I do.'

'He's got 400 Bibles,' says Colonel A, 'so I do.'

'We can't support both,' says the chairman, 'this is always the problem in schools; there are too many worthy causes for the money to go round. I think we'd better vote on this now. Those in favour of granting the request of the RE Department for an extra £250 cash.'

The late arrival leans forward intently.

Dr C and Lady B both show. The chairman (who has the right to vote) includes himself.

'Those against.' Mrs D and Colonel A show. So does the head-master, perhaps through fear of bombardment with similar requests from other departments if the motion is carried.

Three for, three against. But they've forgotten the late arrival. The chairman turns to him and says, 'It looks as if this is really a vote about the whole aims and ethos of RE here. How do you vote, Mr Reader?'

Dear Mr Reader,

We wonder whether you recognize yourself sitting in the governors' meeting there, and how you would vote. We believe that the future of RE lies with you and in how informed you are

about it, and on what you think its aims should be. Our views on
the aims of RE are of course represented by Dr C and Lady B.

We think that bad teaching and misguided aims have done more
to undermine RE than all the arguments of the so-called militant
godless. Of course we can operate in only one small patch – you,
Mr Reader, come from a wider area and carry more influence.
Maybe you agree with Mrs D that RE is on the way out. But
have you heard about some of the developments in RE on the
national scene? The work of the Lancaster (Schools Council)
Project whose aims for RE were called as evidence in chapter 5
has been most welcome. Their clear analysis of the different
reasons for RE teaching is also useful. But the raison d'être of
the Project is the set of units for classroom use. These were produced with the help of serving teachers and they come with
suggestions for teaching, and with clearly defined objectives. The
whole project was worked out from 1969-1972 and takes the
view that the RE teacher should equip pupils with the tools for
a study of religious issues and phenomena. They echo and emphasize
what was said by *The Fourth R* (SPCK 1970), the late Bishop of
Durham's report on RE, and what we have strongly urged, namely
that RE should have at least two periods per week on the timetable.

Not all RE fits Colonel A's view of the aims, or Mrs D's, or
ours; the problem seems to be that a lot of what goes on is aimless,
as people try to survive the hectic day to day business of teaching
without asking what it's all about. A refreshing contrast, therefore,
is, for instance, the Lancaster units, whose aims are clearly defined
at the start.

Not only are the Lancaster kits useful in their own right, their
methodology and outlook should be a useful guide to all RE
teachers planning new courses and syllabuses. They are a 'must'
for teachers and student teachers.

The Schools Council Moral Education Curriculum Project had
an off-spin in the form of the *Lifeline Project* (Longmans 1972), for
classroom use. This is a non-religious examination of human
relationships based on a series of case studies. The book *In Other
People's Shoes* (see acknowledgments) sets out the scheme as
follows:

Purpose: To help boys and girls between the ages of eleven
and sixteen recognize and understand other people's needs, feelings and interests in inter-personal situations and to take those

needs, feelings and interests into consideration when taking action which affects others.

Hypothesis: When an adolescent has considered a situation involving him and one other person, not only from his own point of view but also from that of the other person, he will produce a more considerate answer to the question, 'What shall I do in this situation?' than if he had only looked at that situation from his own point of view. It is further suggested that this increased sensitivity and consideration will carry over into real-life situations and that the subject may, with practice, be able to understand the needs, feelings and interests of two persons in conflict, both of whom are strangers to him and remote from him.

Method: This material consists of real life situations which can be used in a variety of ways depending on the particular interests and abilities of teacher and children.

The sort of situations the groups are asked to discuss include :
Your father is critical of your hair and of your clothes.
You are laughing at a film which is supposed to be serious when an elderly man tells you to be quiet.
E. Situation 57

Middle-aged man (to his friend who looks surprised but does not reply) I'm sorry I smashed your car up, but I was drunk and I couldn't help it.

How would you set about persuading the man who has smashed the car that he could help it?

This sort of situation can be used very successfully with slow learners or ROSLA children. Teachers who have tried it will know that it isn't the easy substitute for conventional teaching that it at first appears; the courtship questions, if used, require very delicate handling, to give but one example.

The Christian Education Movement was one of the pioneers in updating RE. Their material for school use is to be recommended, along with their journal *Learning for Living*, which provides a forum for RE teachers in all types of school and also for more general topics such as counselling. Perhaps of all their services to teachers and students the most useful is the set of RE Service Papers which include such things as O and A level booklists, assembly resources, information for intending RE students etc.

The Association for Religious Education is also doing valuable work to raise the status of RE: they too publish a Bulletin and Papers on aspects of RE, e.g., their survey of the film resources for RE. They have also submitted evidence to various groups looking at the problems or future of RE, such as the Secretary of State – in this case in connection with the proposed new Education Act.

We also welcome the recent formation of RE Resources Centres, one at Borough Road College, London, another at Westhill College, Birmingham, the National Centre at St Gabriel's College, London, with its branch at St John's College, York and others; these should play a valuable role in disseminating new materials and ideas to those teaching RE either full-time or as a second subject, and provide a forum for discussion.

The Pictorial Charts Educational Trust continues to produce first rate wall charts for RE. They have a strong visual impact and their detail makes a good advertisement for children to read outside the classroom lesson time. Secondary schools have sometimes been very slow to learn from primary schools that what is on the wall does matter; PCET ensure that RE has no excuse in this respect.

Even so, the public image of RE leaves a lot to be desired. We should like to see more careers' teachers suggesting to children the possibilities in RE teaching. The present shortage in RE almost guarantees employment and to anyone with any interest and aptitude in the subject it can only be a most interesting and challenging job, particularly now that techniques and syllabuses are being revised and improved. Too often children have been advised into, say, history, because careers' teachers have felt that to advise them into RE is somehow like advising someone to be ordained, almost a trespass into the realms of someone's personal devotion. If – as we hope – the vicar image of the RE teacher is going, there is no guilt to be attached to talking about RE teaching like any other job. Obviously we don't mean that RE should be seen as something purely mercenary; no teaching job should be seen in that light alone. At the same time it is not evil to think about promotion and prospects, and we are encouraged by the number of schools offering head of RE posts on Scale 4, even scale 5, of the Burnham salary scales.

We should like to see the day when, with due ceremony, the last school teaching RI (for that is what it is) in the Sunday school tradition changes its syllabus. We have a special assembly of thanksgiving designed for this great day. The tide is turning. Courses for retraining are available; so are courses for non-specialist RE teachers who find themselves carrying an increasing load in RE but who have no theological background: e.g., the one year Diploma in RE offered by some universities. External certificates in theology can also be helpful.

So there it is.

'Of making many books there is no end, and much study is wearisome to the flesh' (Ecclesiastes 12.12). RE is not a dead or dying subject – it's very much alive, but it needs an educated public and keen teachers. So, student, teacher, parent, pupil, its future rests with you.

Hope you enjoyed the trip.
Yours very sincerely,
Terence Copley
Donald Easton

APPENDIX I

Select Bibliography

Suggested further reading for the non-specialist

RE Background

There are very few up-to-date and sound books in this area, but these may prove useful:

M. Grimmitt, *What Can I Do in RE?*, Mayhew-McCrimmon 1974.

K. E. Hyde, *Religion and Slow Learners*, SCM Press 1969.

H. F. Mathews, *Revolution in Religious Education*, REP 1966.

　The New RE, Methodist Publishing House 1971.

B. Wigley and R. Pitcher, *From Fear to Faith*, Longmans 1969.

Theological Background

R. Bultmann, *Kerygma and Myth*, I, edited R. H. Fuller, SPCK 1953.

C. H. Dodd, *The Parables of the Kingdom* (revised edition), Fontana 1961.

F. C. Grant, *The Gospels. Their Origin and Growth*, Faber 1957.

J. Jeremias, *The Parables of Jesus* (translated by S. H. Hooke, revised edition), SCM Press 1972.

New Larousse Encyclopaedia of Mythology, Hamlyn 1959.

D. E. Nineham, *Saint Mark*, Penguin 1963

G. von Rad, *Genesis* (translated by J. H. Marks), SCM Press 1961.

Assemblies

C. R. Campling and M. Davies, *Words for Worship*, Edward Arnold 1969.

R. Dingwall, *Assembly Workshop*, Darton, Longman and Todd 1972.

E. Morecambe and E. Wise, *Eric and Ernie*, W. H. Allen 1973.

C. Morris, *What the Papers Didn't Say*, Epworth 1971.

For the practising teacher we would recommend the detailed bibliography which can be bought from the Christian Education Movement (2, Chester House, Muswell Hill, London, N10 1PR).

Other useful addresses are:

The Association for Religious Education, Highcroft House, Crown Lane, Sutton Coldfield, Warks.

Pictorial Charts Educational Trust, 132 Uxbridge Road, London W13 3QU.

APPENDIX II

Glossary to Chapter 3

(For the specialist these pages may be used for fish and chip paper. The non-specialist has his revenge in Appendix III, intended for RE teachers only.)

Who's Who in Chapter 3

PAPIAS
Papias (*c.* AD 60-130) was bishop of Hierapolis in Asia Minor. Little is known of his life, and his book survives only in quotations by the more famous and influential churchmen Irenaeus and Eusebius. But although he didn't make the Top Ten, Papias throws interesting light on gospel transmission and origins in the early church in two famous and tantalizing fragments about the gospels of Mark and Matthew, fragments with which all subsequent scholars working on these gospels have had to come to terms. On the authority of the 'Elder' (and the discussion on who he was could fill a book) Papias says that Mark was Peter's interpreter – we assume Peter spoke Aramaic only – and set down accurately, though not however in order, everything that he (Mark) remembered of the words and actions of the Lord, as told by Peter. He goes on to stress that this was not a connected account. Yet despite this statement almost two thousand years ago, many readers of the gospels through the centuries have persisted in teaching them as chronological biographies, and so have many RE teachers in their approach to classroom work on the life of Christ.

JEREMIAS AND DODD
Both twentieth-century New Testament scholars who worked towards a better understanding of the parables which in their view had suffered, sometimes at the hands of moralizing interpreters, sometimes because their original context had been lost. They tried to recover this origin in the preaching of Jesus that the Kingdom of God had invaded the world in his person and mission, and in a careful study of rabbinic use of parable. See C. H. Dodd, *The Parables of the Kingdom* and J. Jeremias, *The Parables of Jesus* for their analysis of this whole question (see bibliography).

BULTMANN

Rudolph Bultmann, one of the greatest theologians of the twentieth century, helped to pioneer form criticism. This is a method of textual study which can be applied to the gospels in an attempt to recover the original context of units of gospel material in the life and needs of the early Christian community and to see what factors led to their preservation. Some, he suggested, were preserved because of a key line or phrase (e.g. 'The sabbath was made for man, not man for the sabbath') and the surrounding details were of less significance; but most units could be classified according to their 'form' e.g. as pronouncement stories, maxims, myths. This method of approach is explained and assessed by E. B. Redlich in a book entitled *Form Criticism*, Duckworth 1939.

These four people have contributed something absolutely fundamental to an understanding of the life of Jesus and a serious study of the gospels; the repercussions of what they have said have still to reach many syllabuses and classrooms.

APPENDIX III
Addenda to Chapter 6 – Further notes on GCE work

1. *Good O Level notes*
The importance of good notes cannot be overstressed, for on this above all the exam success of GCE candidates depends. A level pupils can be assumed to be mature enough to organize their own notes; O level pupils need help.

Good O level notes incorporate three characteristics: thoroughness, clear headings, periodic summaries. This last is important as an aid to last-minute revision. In the case of textual study there is also a fourth characteristic: the inclusion, but clear separation, of both critical comment and exposition. It always comes as a surprise to new teachers to realize how much O level teaching is taken up by simple explanation of what is recounted in a biblical text.

To illustrate our idea of good notes, we are including some specimen pages from the book of an O level pupil in a class on Acts.

(See pages 116-17)

2. *Planning the Syllabus*
The right choice of syllabus is important. Fortunately, GCE boards are now opening up wider ranges of papers – 'fortunately', because we suffered for so long with nothing but Biblical Studies. We now have Modern Church History and Philosophy of Religion available at A level, and such papers as The Problem of Suffering available at O level. We gratefully accept some of these innovations. On the other hand, we do not approve of the tendency in some quarters to retreat altogether from biblical study. In our view a thorough, critical, beginning-to-end study of at least one biblical book is an essential element in anyone's training in religious study and should be included as a matter of course at some stage in each GCE pupil's career. But in dealing with biblical texts you have to consider the nature of the documents you're going to teach: the Old Testament prophetic books as they now stand are the product of very haphazard editing and collation, most of which took place in the exilic and post-exilic periods. One has to plan a way of making sense of this to one's pupils.

Rearrangement of the text is the best method. Of course any re-arrangement has objections which can be found against it, but we have to live with the fact that there is no such thing as one hundred per cent agreement among scholars; so we must simply take the plunge and do the best we can. At any rate, some structure is better than none. The ideal is for the overall scheme to have a chronological basis (if this is possible) but, within the chronological sections, to be broken up into themes of preaching. One corollary of the chronological arrangement will be that secondary oracles are sieved out from the primary material. These can then be arranged in themes amongst themselves and dealt with at the end; they are valuable in illustrating the growth of prophetic 'schools'.

If rearrangement of the text is the best method, it is also the most demanding. It is no good supposing that the teacher can have his own private list of rearranged passages and can teach his pupils by telling them to jump hither and thither, flipping from page to page in the prophets. This is altogether too confusing and to the pupils it appears aimless. The ideal solution is to rewrite the text entirely, in a rearranged order with headings and subheadings, duplicate it, and give it to the pupils. Failing this, one may duplicate simply a list of headings and references in the order in which they will be taught, and give this to the pupils. If rearranging the text for teaching purposes, you must give your victims a written programme. If you don't, they will never know where they are going or how much ground they have covered.

At this point we are including some lists of this sort. We do not claim one hundred per cent academic respectability for them (we are not professional theologians in that sense), but we do think they are broadly sound. They are included here partly to illustrate the principle we have described, and partly as an aid to those teachers who may not have the time (or inclination) to work out such schemes for themselves. It should be remembered that in what follows, the prime consideration is clarity of presentation.

AMOS: WORK SCHEME

I SUPERSCRIPTION
    1.1.

II THE VISION OF AMOS
    7.1-3, 4-6, 7-9; 8.1-3; 9.1-4.

III THE PREACHING OF AMOS
(1) The great sermon 1.3-2.16; cf.9.7-8.
(2) Critique of Israel (*a*) Affluence 6.1-7; 4.1-3.
                       (*b*) Injustice 5.7, 10-11; 6.12.
                       (*c*) Religion 4.4-5; 5.4-6, 21-24, 25-27.
(3) Iniquity and punishment 3.13-15, 9-11; 6.13-14; 8.4-8.
(4) The past (*a*) Yahweh's favour 3.1-2.
            (*b*) Warnings 4.6-12.

④ Stephen
6:1 - 7:60.

6:1-7) His appointment as one of the seven.
6:8-15) His influence and preaching.
7:-3) His trial and death.

6:1-7) His appointment as one of the seven.

A. Quarrel between the Hellenists and Hebrews.
i) They all held the Jewish faith.
ii) They were also christians.
iii) They all lived in Jerusalem.

Difference
Hellenists came from gentile lands and spoke greek.
Hebrews were natives of Judea and spoke Aramaic.

v-1 The greek speaking woman were not getting as much funds as the aramaic speaking widows. It was the aramaic speaking people who distributed the funds.

v-2 They held a meeting.
{ The twelve mention something else at the meeting. }

They object to administrating the funds because they want to spend more time preaching.

w 5-6 All have greek names those who are chosen for the seven.

v-5. One of the man called Steven.

6:8-15 Stephen's influence and preaching.-

Stephen was appointed to look after the fund but gained fame for his preaching and healing.

v-9. He seems to have done his preaching in the synagogues of Jerusalem, which were attended by the greek speaking Jews.

V-9 Synagogues didn't like what Stephen was saying so they started a rumour.

V-13 The authorities are stirred up and he is brought to trial infront of the Sanhedrin.

CHAPTER 7.

His trial and death. - Stephen's speech

(i) Making his own defence.

Argument—trying to prove that God does not need a temple.

(ii) Attack against his judges

Everybody in Jewish history who has realised that God does not need a temple has been persecuted.

Stephen tries to prove his statement by bringing examples out of Jewish history.

The Jewish history that Stephen refers to.

① Abraham— God called Abraham to be founder of the Jewish race. They believed he had been born in Mesopotamia and

---

V-9 Synagogue of the Freedman were attending Jews living in Jerusalem who were descendants of Jews who were slaves in Rome.

What Stephen preached.

V-11 (i) Moses was the giver of the law so if you blasphemed against Moses you were insulting the Jewish Law.

VV-13,14 (ii) Holy place = the temple.

False witness' said that Stephen was saying that Jesus would destroy the temple and change the law.

No need for temple (temple used for sacrifice) because Jesus had been sacrificed and that was enough to bring God closer to them forever. The Jews believed that sacrifice brought you closer to God.

(iii) Stephen makes a speech and one of his main themes in his speech is that God does not need a temple.

I:

Pages from an O Level note book.

(5) An appeal to Israel 5.14-15.

(6) The day of Yahweh 3.1-2; 5.18-20; 3.12; 6.8-11; 8.9-14; 5.1-3, 12-13, 16-17.

(7) Amos defends his ministry 1.2; 3.3-8.

IV THE END OF AMOS' MINISTRY
7.10-17.

V SOME HYMNS
4.13; 5.8-9; 9.5-6.

VI HOPE FOR THE FUTURE
9.9-15.

HOSEA : WORK SCHEME

I SUPERSCRIPTION
1.1.

II THE MARRIAGE THEME

(1) Hosea's enacted prophecies 1.2-9; 3.1-4 (+5).

(2) Yahweh divorces Israel 2.2-13.

III CRITIQUE OF ISRAEL

(1) Summary 4.1-3; 6.7-7.2.

(2) Apostasy 4.15-19; 5.3-7; 11.12-12.4.

(3) The cult 4.11-14; 7.13-16; 10.1-15; 13.1-3.

(4) Priests 4.4-10.

(5) Kings and leaders 5.1-2; 7.3-7; 13.10-11.

IV PUNISHMENT

(1) By Yahweh 13.4-9; 9.1-17.

(2) By the nations 5.8-6.6; 7.8-12; 8.1-14.

V YAHWEH'S LOVE FOR ISRAEL

(1) Yahweh as father 11.1-9.

(2) Salvation oracles 1.10-2.1; 2.14-22; 11.10-11; 13.14.

(3) Israel's return 14.1-8.

VI EPILOGUE
14.9.

ISAIAH 1-12; 28-39 : WORK SCHEME

Part I ISAIAH OF JERUSALEM

I SUPERSCRIPTION
1.1.

II THE INAUGURAL VISION
6.1-13.

III ISAIAH'S CRITIQUE OF CONTEMPORARY SOCIETY

(1) The central issue 1.2-3.

(2) The alternatives 1.18-20.

(3) The probable outcome 5.13-17.
(4) The parable of the vineyard 5.1-7.
(5) Social injustice and Yahweh's judgment on it 5.8-10, 11-12, 18-23;
10.1-4; 3.1-5, 6-8, 9-12, 13-15, 16-17, 18-4.1.
(6) Judah's worship and Yahweh's judgment on it 1.10-11, 12-17;
28.13; 5.24.

IV ISAIAH AND THE SYRO-EPHRAIMITE CRISIS, 735-734 BC
(1) Call to trust in Yahweh 7.1-16; 7.21; 8.9-10.
(2) The alternative 8.5-6; 8.1-4; 10.22-23.
(3) Oracles concerning the Northern Kingdom 2.5-19; 9.8-12, 13-17,
18-21; 5.25, 26-29.

V ISAIAH AND THE ASSYRIAN CRISIS, 701 BC
(*A*) *Events leading up to it, and Isaiah's warnings*
(1) Yahweh's plan to destroy Judah 29.1-6; 1.21-26; 31-4; 7.20, 25;
28.20-22; 10.33-34; 10.28,32.
(2) Assyria's boastfulness 10.5-15; 14.24-27.
(3) Alliances with Babylon and Egypt 39.1-5; 31.1-3; 30.1-5, 6-7.
(4) Call to trust in Yahweh 14.28-32; 8.11-15; 28.16-17; 17.12-14; 8.1-6;
30.27-28, 29-33.
(5) Consequences of Judah's rejection of Yahweh 28.7-13, 14-19;
10.16-19; 30.8-17.

(*B*) *The Events of 701 BC (Historical Accounts)*
(1) The deliverance tradition (i) 36.1-22; 37.1-9a, 37-38.
            (ii) 37.9b-36.
            (iii) is supported by a tradition of Heze-
                  kiah's piety 38.1-7; 38.9-20.
(2) The defeat tradition (i) II Kings 18.13-16.
            (ii) Sennacherib's account. See the Taylor
                  Prism.

(*C*) *Isaiah's Preaching in 701 BC*
1.4-9; 22.1-8, 9-11, 12-14.

Part II THE GROWTH OF THE ISAIAH TRADITION

I THE DELIVERANCE TRADITION
(1) Prophecies of deliverance 29.5-8; 31.5, 8-9; 28.23-29; 30.18; 37.30.
(2) A taunt-song against Assyria 37.22-29.
(3) Writing the history (references as above).
(4) Deliverance as a theme in liturgy 33.1-24; 12.1-6.
(5) A source of hopes for the future
    (i) A new remnant 37.31; 10.20; 28.5-6.
    (ii) Return from exile and dispersion 10.24-27; 11.11-16; 35.1-10.
    (iii) Yahweh's vengeance on the nation 34.1-17.

II THE DEFEAT TRADITION

(1) Writing the history (references as above).

(2) Isaiah's critique reapplied to depict the future 1.27-31; 31.6-7; 2.20-22; 4.2-6; 29.17-21.

III THE NEW AGE

(1) Yahweh will reawaken his people's faith 30.19-26; 29.22-24; 32.15-20.

(2) The Ideal King 9.1-7; 11.10; 11.1-9; 32.1-8.

(3) Israel a centre of pilgrimage 7.18; 2.1-4.

V THE BOOK

A legend of its origin and an assessment of its importance 8.16-22.

JEREMIAH 1-49: WORK SCHEME
(selected passages)

I THE CALL
  1.4-10, 11-12, 17-19.

II JEREMIAH'S PREACHING

(A) *Destruction from the North*

(1) Spoken oracles 1.13-16; 4.5-18, 23-26; 5.14-17; 6.1-8, 22-26.

(2) Enacted prophecies 13.1-11, 12-14; 18.1-12; 19.1-2, 10-11a, 14-15.

(B) *Judah's faithlessness*

(1) The Covenant 11.1-17.

(2) Faithlessness 2.1-13, 18-37; 3.1-5, 19-25; 4.1-4; 9.25-26; 13.20-27; 17.1-4.

(3) The cult 5.30-31; 8.8-13; 7.21-24.

(C) *The Temple Sermon*
  7.1-15.

III JEREMIAH AND THE FALL OF JERUSALEM

(A) *The Siege in 598* BC
  Attitude to exiles 24.1-10; 27.1-28.17; 29.1-32.

(B) *The Siege in 588* BC

(1) Slaves 34.1-22.

(2) Jeremiah 37.3-21.

(3) Hope for the future 30.1-31.40.

(4) Jeremiah 38.1-28.

(C) *The Fall, and after*
  39.1-44.30.

IV JEREMIAH AND HIS VOCATION

(A) *Attitude to his task*
  6.27-30; 4.19-22; 8.18-9.3; 7.16-20; 11.14; 14.11-12; 7.25-28; 16.1-9.

(B) Relation to other prophets
   14.13-16; 27.1-28.17; 23.9-33; 29.16-19; 34.1-7.
   Also Deuteronomy 18.9-22; 13.1-5.

(C) Opposition
   11.18-23; 20.1-6; 37.11-21; 38.1-13; 15.10-21.

(D) Doubt
   12.1-6; 18.18-23; 17.5-18; 20.7-18.

V JEREMIAH AND HIS BOOK
   45.1-5; 36.1-32.

For the gospels, or Acts, a different type of scheme is needed. These books have built-in plans, unlike the prophets, because each one is far more the work of an individual. For this reason a beginning-to-end study can be more successful with these books, provided the natural scheme of the book is made clear. Some people find it helpful, when teaching the gospels, to deal with certain matters by themes; thus all miracle stories are dealt with at one blow, and similarly all parables and all opposition stories. There really seems little to choose between the two methods. One follows the plan of the evangelist, the other the plan of the teacher. The main thing is that there should be a plan. The one New Testament book where rearrangement would be essential is I and II Corinthians; fortunately this confused text is not generally prescribed for GCE study.

If the built-in plan is being followed, it can be helpful to pupils if the plan is made absolutely dominant. This may mean making slight rearrangements of the text where the main outline of the book is less clear. This applies notably to Acts, for which the following scheme can be used.

ACTS: WORK SCHEME

PRELUDE
(1) Luke's introduction 1.1-2a.
(2) Events between the Resurrection and the Ascension 1.2b-11.
(3) Waiting in Jerusalem 1.12-14.
(4) The election of Matthias 1.15-26.

I THE CHURCH IN JERUSALEM
(1) Pentecost 2.1-42.
(2) Church life 4.32-37; 2.45-47; 5.1-11.
(3) Healings, trials and imprisonments 3.1-4.31; 5.12-42; 12.1-19.
(4) Stephen 6.1-7.60.

(5) Persecution 8.1-3.
(6) Death of Herod Agrippa I 12.20-24.

II THE MISSION INTO PALESTINE
(1) Philip 8.4-40.
(2) Peter 9.32-11.18.

III THE MISSION TO ASIA MINOR AND GREECE
Part (i)
(1) Conversion of Saul 9.1-31.
(2) Church in Antioch 11.19-30.
(3) Paul's first journey 12.25-14.28.
(4) Council of Jerusalem 15.1-35.
Part (ii) Paul's journeys 15.36-21.16, especially covering: Philippi, Athens, Corinth, Ephesus, Troas, Miletus.

IV CHRISTIANITY REACHES ROME
(1) Riot in Jerusalem 21.17-23.10.
(2) Paul's escape to Caesarea 23.11-35.
(3) Paul's trials 24.1-26.52 (Felix, Festus, Herod Agrippa II).
(4) Journey to Rome 27.1-28.16.
(5) Paul in Rome 28.17-31.

Non-biblical papers do not pose such problems for the O or A level teacher, as a simple teaching-scheme can usually be drawn up through careful study of previous exam questions. It might be added that there are enormous practical advantages if the teacher keeps a card index of past GCE questions. During a busy term much time can otherwise be wasted searching through past papers for appropriate essay titles.

3. *Revision*

Using revision both to maintain morale and to ensure that the pupils get to grips with their material is always difficult. But a number of principles can be suggested.

1. Two months before the exam all regular teaching should stop. Whatever is untaught should remain untaught. Pupils should not be submerged under a last-minute avalanche of new material.

2. Close attention must be given to the pupils' own preferred methods of revision, although suggestions and advice from the teacher will be important. By this time even recalcitrant pupils will usually be conscientious, so allow some latitude for them to work in the way that they say helps them most.

3. Pupils must be given a detailed knowledge of what sorts of questions they are likely to be faced with. At this stage go all-out for exammanship.

4. There should be frequent, regular and careful checking on each pupil's progress during the revision period. This really means that there should be tests.

5. All tests should be marked and handed back with the maximum possible speed. This provides the pupils with an immediate 'feedback' and so gives immediate reward or disappointment. It also permits bad revision techniques to be spotted and remedied before they do too much harm.

6. Tests should not usually be on large topics (e.g. the whole of the Fourth Gospel) but on small, manageable portions.

7. The overall programme for revision should be imposed on the pupils by the teacher, after careful explanation and discussion. Left to themselves pupils will inevitably fall behind in their revision plans, so it is the teacher's job to insist that the programme is adhered to.

How these principles are put into practice will vary from teacher to teacher and class to class. But here are some methods which we found helpful at Hinchingbrooke. All pupils are given duplicated sheets containing questions from past exam papers. O level pupils need a very close knowledge of biblical texts (if this is the paper being offered), and are therefore given every gobbet (i.e. 'context-question') set during the past five or seven years. They are also given a clean exercise book in which to do fair copies of as many gobbets as they can during their spare time. Gobbet-books are taken in and inspected from time to time.

A level pupils need to learn how to adapt the knowledge they possess to answer a wide range of possible questions. Their list, therefore, contains summaries of all questions asked on each topic during the past seven years. Lists of gobbetable passages of text can also be given. We include here an example of the sort of list in question. The reader will notice that there is no indication of the incidence of individual questions. This is because we consider it very risky to encourage detailed 'question-spotting'. The practice is only of use in its most general form. For example, it would be worth knowing that there was generally a question on some aspect of nineteenth-century Anglo-Catholicism; but any more precise prediction would most probably run aground.

MODERN CHURCH HISTORY:
Exam Topics (A level check-list)

1. Condition of the Church of England in 1830, Peel's Commission, its effect. Who really saved the Church of England: Peel or the Oxford Movement?

2. The Evangelical Movement
Its impact within Church of England.
Shaftesbury.

3. Nonconformity
Why did it grow between 1830-1900?
Why did Methodism split up in the century after Wesley?
The Keswick Convention
William Booth

4. Roman Catholicism
Why did it grow in England after 1850?
First Vatican Council: was Pius IX realistic?
Catholic Modernism: Loisy
Second Vatican Council: is it a new Reformation?
John XXIII
Comparision of Vatican I with Vatican II

5. The Broad Church Movement
S. T. Coleridge
Thomas Arnold

6. Christian Socialism
F. D. Maurice
Has the role of Christians in the Labour movement been exaggerated?

7. Oxford Movement, leading into Ritualism
Was it reaction against liberalism?
Was it 'academic, clerical, and conservative'?
Why did Newman abandon the *via media*?
How did Anglo-Catholicism change after 1845?
Charles Gore
The Public Worship Regulation Act, and why it failed
Is it true that there were 'martyrs of ritualism'?
The twentieth-century liturgical revival and its effect

8. Christianity and Science
Reasons for growth of doubt *before* Darwin
Why did people lose their faith in the nineteenth century?
How geology changed traditional views of Genesis
Why *The Origin of Species* disturbed some Christians

What happened at the British Association meeting in 1860?
Why did Marx and Freud treat religion as an illusion?
Is there still a conflict between science and religion?

9. The Bible
Essays and Reviews
Was scholarship more unsettled over the NT than over the OT in the
nineteenth century?
Why was the RV produced? Is it a good translation?

10. Education
Differences in ideas and achievements between National Society and
British and Foreign School Society.
Why 'the religious question' was solved in 1944 but not in 1902

11. Mission and Ecumenism
Nineteenth-century missions, and their link with anti-slavery movements
Were nineteenth-century missionaries agents of Imperialism?
Twentieth-century missions: how are they different from nineteenth-
    century missions?
Problems for the church in newly independent countries
Influence of missionary concerns on ecumenical movement
Edinburgh Conference of 1910
The Ecumenical Movement since 1910
The World Council of Churches
Has Christianity become more tolerant of other religions? If so, why?

12. Nazi Germany and Modern Theology
Problems posed for the churches by Nazism
Karl Barth: theologian and twentieth-century prophet?
Bultmann's theology
Bonhoeffer's career and influence
Honest to God: why did it sell so quickly?

13. Urban Evangelism
What steps did the churches take in this direction 1830-1914?
Why have the churches not touched the working classes?

14. General
Religion in the Victorian novel
Influence of hymns

For all GCE pupils every lesson brings a test. For O level pupils
this is on not more than two chapters of text; for A level pupils it is
on one pre-selected topic. O level pupils are tested with a quick series
of twenty short questions, which are corrected immediately in class.
Test essays should not be used here as they permit more waffle and
take longer to mark. To A level pupils, however, test essays are given.

The issue is known in advance, but not the precise form of the question. In this way they gain practice in manipulating a limited body of knowledge to suit the needs of the occasion.

Most A level students like to make revision notes. This is the biggest demand on their time in the earlier weeks of revision. So revision notes should be insisted upon for each topic due to be tested. They should be inspected, and the test essays should be marked, and they should all be handed back at the very next lesson. This is a heavy burden on the teacher, but it pays dividends.

Index

Index

Agreed Syllabus 51
Aims 10, 60f, 63-69, 84, 93, 103-107
Assemblies 1-13
Association for Religious Education 108f, 111

Baker, Chief Inspector 50, 81
Street 50
Bible 22, 30, 43f, 86, 97ff, 104
Bultmann 18-20, 50f, 113

Christ, life of 18-20, 21f, 48f, 55, 97
Christian Education Movement, 108, 111
Church:
early 20ff
history 60, 61-67
modern 20, 124f
tradition 22, 98
CSE 79-91
syllabus 85-87

Discussions 55
Dodd 23f, 50f, 112
Drama 42f, 94f, 96

Examinations:
CSE 79-91
CSE syllabus 85-87
GCE A level 92-102
GCE A level syllabus 114-122
GCE O level 92-102, 114-117
GCE O level syllabus 121f
GCE O level syllabus (Introductory) 97-99

internal 70-75
revision 100f, 122-126

Fifth year 80-91, 92-102
See also examinations, CSE & GCE
First year 10-13, 26f
syllabus 28-31
Form criticism 18f, 113
Fourth year 53-78, 79-91
See also examinations, CSE & GCE

GCE See examinations

Jeremias 23f, 50f, 112

Lancaster Project 84, 107
Lifeline 107f
Lower school 10-13, 14-52

Methods 42-44, 46f, 96f, 101f
Middle school 53-78, 79-91, 92-102
See also examinations, CSE & GCE
Moral education 29f, 55f, 63-67, 88f, 90, 107f
Myth 26f, 28f

Old Testament 26f, 28-31, 42, 114-121

Papias 17f, 50f, 112
Parables 21, 23f, 112
Projects 12f, 77, 85-87